Houghton Mifflin Science
DiscoveryWorks

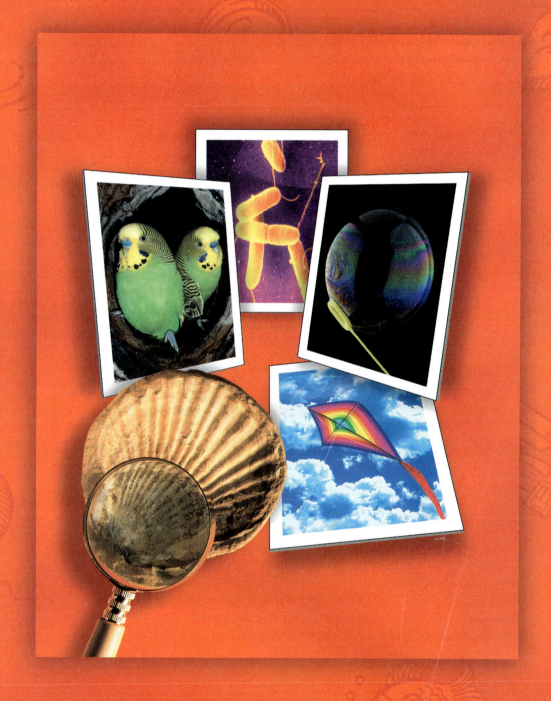

HOUGHTON MIFFLIN

Boston • Atlanta • Dallas • Denver • Geneva, Illinois • Palo Alto • Princeton

Authors

William Badders
Elementary Science Teacher
Cleveland Public Schools
Cleveland, OH

Lowell J. Bethel
Professor of Science Education
The University of Texas at Austin
Austin, TX

Victoria Fu
Professor of Child Development
and Early Childhood Education
Virginia Polytechnic Institute and
State University
Blacksburg, VA

Donald Peck
Director (retired)
The Center for Elementary Science
Fairleigh Dickinson University
Madison, NJ

Carolyn Sumners
Director of Astronomy and Physical Sciences
Houston Museum of Natural Science
Houston, TX

Catherine Valentino
Author-in-Residence, Houghton Mifflin
West Kingston, RI

Acknowledgements appear on page H24, which constitutes an extension of this copyright page.

Copyright © 2000 by Houghton Mifflin Company. All rights reserved.

No part of this work may be reproduced or transmitted in any form or by any means, electronic or mechanical, including photocopying or recording, or by any information storage or retrieval system without the prior written permission of Houghton Mifflin Company unless such copying is expressly permitted by federal copyright law. Address inquiries to School Permissions, 222 Berkeley Street, Boston, MA 02116.

Printed in the U. S. A.

ISBN 0-618-00827-6

5 6 7 8 9 10 RRD 08 07 06 05 04 03 02 01

CONTENTS

THINK LIKE A SCIENTIST
Floating and Sinking S2
Reading to Learn S8
Safety S10

UNIT A
Life Cycles — A–A55

UNIT B
Energy and Motion — B–B51

UNIT C
Earth's Materials — C–C57

UNIT D
What Makes Me Sick — D–D41

SCIENCE and MATH TOOLBOX H1–H9
Glossary H10
Index H18
Credits H24

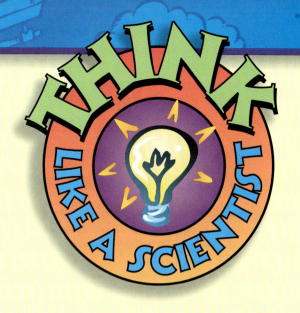

Floating and Sinking S2
Observe S2
Ask a Question S3
Make a Hypothesis S4
Plan and Do a Test S5
Record What Happens S6
Draw Conclusions S7

Reading to Learn S8

Safety S10

Floating and Sinking

A scientist thinks about ideas in a careful way. You too, can think like a scientist.

Observe

To think like a scientist, **observe** the things around you. Everything you hear and see is a clue about how the world works.

Roland and Shannon are playing with clay. They make the clay into many shapes. Roland places a clay ball into water. The clay ball sinks. Why did this happen?

Ask a Question

As you observe, you may see that some things happen over and over. **Ask questions** about such things.

Roland says that the clay ball is too heavy to float. Shannon points out that heavy boats float. How can Roland and Shannon change the clay so it will float?

Make a Hypothesis

Suppose you have an idea about why something happens. You make a **hypothesis**, or a guess based on your idea.

Shannon has an idea about what made the clay ball sink. She thinks that changing the shape of the clay might make the clay float. What do you think?

Plan and Do a Test

After you make a hypothesis, **plan** how to **test** it. Then carry out your plan.

Roland and Shannon test the idea. Roland makes the clay ball into a boat. The boat has space inside it. He puts the boat in water. Will it float?

Record What Happens

You need to observe your test carefully. Then **record**, or write down, what happens.

Roland and Shannon watch the clay boat. They see that it floats. Shannon records what they did and what happened. What did she write?

Draw Conclusions

Think about reasons why something happened as it did. Then **draw conclusions**.

Roland decides that the shape of the boat and the space inside help it float. The clay ball did not have a space inside and so the ball could not float. Try it!

Reading to Learn

Before You Read

1. **Look** at the pictures.
2. **Read** the words.
3. **Read** the title.
4. **Look** at the **new words**.

Scientists read to have fun and to learn. You can, too! Just follow these steps.

Seeds grow better when they have room to grow. Some seeds are carried away from their parent plants by wind or water. Animals also help move seeds. Sometimes seeds stick to an animal's fur. Some animals, such as birds and squirrels, eat fruits and carry seeds to a new location.

✓ **Reading Check** **Write a story** about a seed that grows into a new plant.

LESSON 7 RESOURCE A35

While You Read

1. **Read** the words carefully.
2. **Look** at the pictures again.
3. **Ask** for help if you need it.

After You Read

1. **Tell** what you have learned.
2. **Show** what you have learned.

SAFETY

Wear your goggles when your teacher tells you.

Handle materials carefully.

Never put things into your mouth.

Wash your hands after every activity.

Always tell an adult if you are hurt.

Be kind to living things.

Clean up spills.

Save resources and materials to use again.

Throw out materials you can't use again.

UNIT A

Life Cycles

Theme: Constancy and Change

LESSON 1 What is a life cycle?
- **Activity** Looking at Animal Families A2
- **Resource** Changes in Living Things A4

LESSON 2 What are the stages in an animal's life?
- **Activity** Examining Eggs A8
- **Resource** The Life Cycle of a Bird A10

LESSON 3 How do animal life cycles differ?
- **Activity** Observing a Mealworm A12
- **Resource** Different Animal Life Cycles A14

LESSON 4 What do living things inherit from their parents?
- **Activity** Training a Goldfish A16
- **Resource** Inherited or Learned? A18

Checkpoint A20

Lesson 5 — What are the stages in a plant's life cycle?
Activity   Collecting Clues of Plant Life Cycles . . A22
Resource   The Life Cycle of a Plant A24

Lesson 6 — Where do some plants form seeds?
Activity   Examining Flowers and Fruits A26
Resource   Flowers and Fruits A28

Lesson 7 — How do new plants begin to grow?
Activity   Examining a Seed A32
Resource   A Seed Is a Beginning A34

Lesson 8 — What things can affect how plants grow?
Activity   Observing Growing Plants A36
Resource   How Plants Adapt A38

Lesson 9 — How are living things of one kind different?
Activity   Comparing Fruits A42
Resource   The Same, but Not the Same A44

Lesson 10 — What things can affect a life cycle?
Activity   Washing Away the Soil A48
Resource   Good or Bad? A50

Unit Review A52

Using Reading Skills A54

Using Math Skills A55

LESSON 1: What is a life cycle?

Activity
Looking at Animal Families

What You Need

animal cards

crayons

Science Notebook

1 (Using Math) **Sort** the animal cards. Put the babies in one group. Put the adults in another group.

2 **Match** each baby animal with its parent. **Tell** how you decided. **Record** your groups.

LIFE CYCLES

❸ **Talk about** how each baby is like or different from its parent. **Record** your ideas.

Looking at Animal Families		
Animal	How baby and parent are alike	How baby and parent are different

Think! How do different animals change throughout their life?

Internet Field Trip

Visit **www.eduplace.com** to see how animals change as they grow.

LESSON 1 ACTIVITY

Changes in Living Things

This woodland is full of living things. All living things go through changes in their lifetime.

The changes happen in steps, or **stages**. These ordered stages are called a **life cycle**. Different plants and animals have different life cycles. A life cycle is like a circle. It has no end.

Find the baby animals in the picture. There are seven different kinds. How are they alike? How are they different? All baby animals grow and change as they get older. As baby animals grow and change, they become **adult** animals.

What will these animals look like when they become adults? What do you think the parents of these baby animals look like? Turn the page to find out.

Which baby animals look like their parents? The squirrels, the birds, the snakes, the deer, and the bobcats look like their parents.

Which babies look different than their parents? The tadpoles are baby frogs. They don't look much like their parents. Tadpoles go through many changes as they grow. What other animal babies look different than their parents?

Most baby animals look much like the other babies of their kind. Baby squirrels look like adult squirrels. They also look like each other. Tadpoles do not look like frogs. But they do look like each other. Do you think the tadpoles will look like each other when they grow up to be frogs?

Reading Check **Write a story** about how an animal changes from a baby to an adult.

LESSON 2: What are the stages in an animal's life?

Activity
Examining Eggs

What You Need

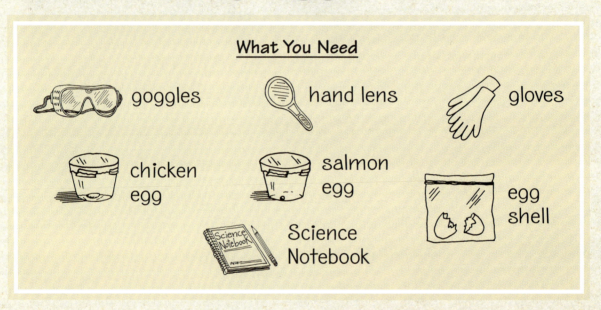

- goggles
- hand lens
- gloves
- chicken egg
- salmon egg
- egg shell
- Science Notebook

1 Use a hand lens. **Look at** the chicken egg. Look for different parts. **Record** what you see.

❷ Now **look at** the shell of the chicken egg. Look for different parts. **Record** what you see.

❸ **Look at** the salmon egg. **Record** what you see.

❹ **Compare** the parts of the chicken egg and the salmon egg.

Think! How are the eggs different? Why are they different?

A mother bird lays eggs in her nest.

The baby bird grows into an adult.

The Life Cycle of a Bird

An **egg** is the first stage in the life cycle of most animals. Some animal babies grow from eggs inside their mother's bodies. Those babies are born live.

Other babies grow from eggs outside their mother's bodies. Those babies break out of their eggs or **hatch**.

The baby birds grow inside the eggs. Then they hatch from the eggs.

The parents feed the babies in the nest.

The baby birds grow feathers and leave the nest.

A mother bird lays its eggs in a safe place. The baby bird grows inside the egg. The food it needs is inside the egg, too. Then it hatches from the egg. Over time, the baby bird grows into an adult bird. The life cycle begins again when the adult bird has babies. Remember, a life cycle has no end. The life cycle goes on and on.

Reading Check Write about the stages in the life cycle of an animal you know.

LESSON 3 How do animal life cycles differ?

Activity
Observing a Mealworm

What You Need

- goggles
- container A with mealworms
- container B
- hand lens
- spoon
- slices of apple or potato
- Science Notebook

1 Use a hand lens to **observe** the mealworms in container A. **Record** what you see.

❷ Look for mealworms in the shape of a C. Use a spoon to move the C-shaped mealworms to container B.

❸ **Using Math** Every two days, **observe** the mealworms in both containers. Move any C-shaped mealworms to container B. **Record** what you see. Put a fresh slice of food in container A.

Think! How does a mealworm change?

Find Out More!

Earthworms have the same body shape as mealworms. Do they grow and change in the same way? Make a plan to find out.

LESSON 3 ACTIVITY   A13

mouse

butterfly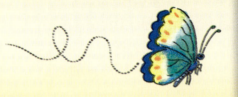

frog

Different Animal Life Cycles

Different kinds of animals grow in different ways. The stages of their life cycles are different.

A baby mouse is born live. It looks a lot like the adult. As a mouse grows, it grows fur and gets bigger. Its fur changes from gray to brown as it grows. How else does a mouse change?

How are the life cycles of a butterfly and a frog alike? They both change form as they grow. A caterpillar hatches from a butterfly egg. It changes form and becomes a butterfly. A tadpole hatches from a frog egg. It changes form and becomes a frog. How does an animal's life cycle begin again?

Reading Check Choose two animals. **Tell** how the life cycles of the animals are alike and different.

Lesson 4: What do living things inherit from their parents?

Activity

Training a Goldfish

What You Need
- 2 goldfish in a fish tank
- fish food
- signal
- Science Notebook

① Put a signal into the water at one end of the tank. Move it up and down ten times. **Observe** and **record** what the fish do. Later in the day, feed the fish at the other end of the tank.

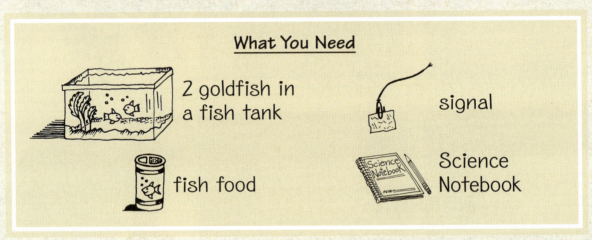

Training a Goldfish	
Day	What fish do
1	
2	
3	

LIFE CYCLES

❷ The next day, repeat step 1 but feed the fish in the center of the tank.

❸ **Using Math** On the third day, move the signal up and down in the water ten times. Then sprinkle food where the signal is. **Observe** and **record** what the fish do.

❹ Repeat step 3 for four more days.

❺ On the eighth day, move the signal up and down in the water ten times. Do not feed the fish. **Observe** and **record** what the fish do.

Think! What did the goldfish learn to do?

LESSON 4 ACTIVITY

Inherited or Learned?

Living things get, or **inherit**, traits from their parents. The squirrels and the puppies inherited their body shapes and fur colors from their parents.

Changes in the environment can affect these animals. In a cold winter, their fur may become thicker. Their fur would get thinner again in the hot summer.

Some things are not passed on from parents to babies. These things are **learned**. The girl is learning to ride a bicycle. She was not born knowing how to do that. The dog has learned how to sit and beg. The squirrels have learned to get food from a bird feeder. What other things can living things learn?

Reading Check **Draw a picture** to show two things you inherited and two things you have learned.

UNIT A CHECKPOINT

Word Power

If you need help, turn to the pages shown in blue.

Match the words with a picture. (A4–A5, A10–A11)

egg   life cycle   hatch

1.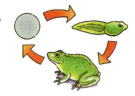
2.
3.

Use these words to fill in the blanks.

learned   adult   inherit   stages

4. Reading is something that is _____ . (A18–A19)
5. The steps of a life cycle are called _____ . (A4–A5)
6. Baby animals _____ their body coverings from their parents. (A18–A19)
7. Baby animals grow and change into _____ animals. (A4–A5)

Solving Science Problems

Match each baby animal with its parent. Tell how you decided.

People Using Science

Guide Dog Instructor

Guide dog instructors train dogs to help people who are blind. They also teach blind people how to use their guide dogs.

The dogs learn how to guide blind people down the sidewalk. They also learn how to safely guide a person across a street. What traits might a guide dog inherit?

 ## Using a Table

Hatching Eggs							
Day	Sun.	Mon.	Tues.	Wed.	Thur.	Fri.	Sat.
Number of eggs	10	25	19	17	23	14	8

Use the table to answer the questions.

1. How many eggs hatched on Tuesday?
2. How many eggs hatched on Sunday?
3. How many eggs hatched on Monday and Thursday altogether?
4. How many more eggs hatched on Wednesday than on Friday?

CHECKPOINT A21

Lesson 5: What are the stages in a plant's life cycle?

Activity
Collecting Clues of Plant Life Cycles

What You Need

- grocery bag
- hand lens
- Science Notebook

1. Take a walk with your class. **Look** for clues that plants change as they grow. Put items you find in a bag.

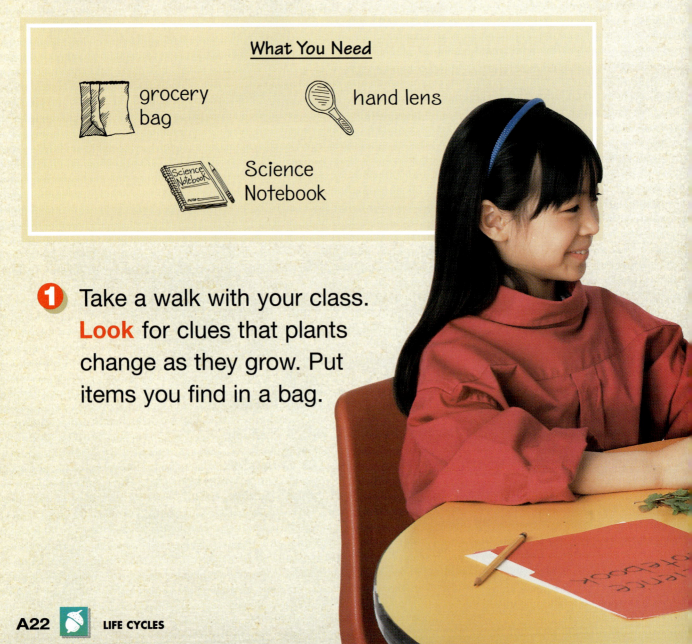

❷ **Look at** each item with a hand lens. Think about which stage of the life cycle the item shows.

❸ Choose two different items. **Record** how you think each item has changed or will change.

Think! How do plant life cycles compare with animal life cycles?

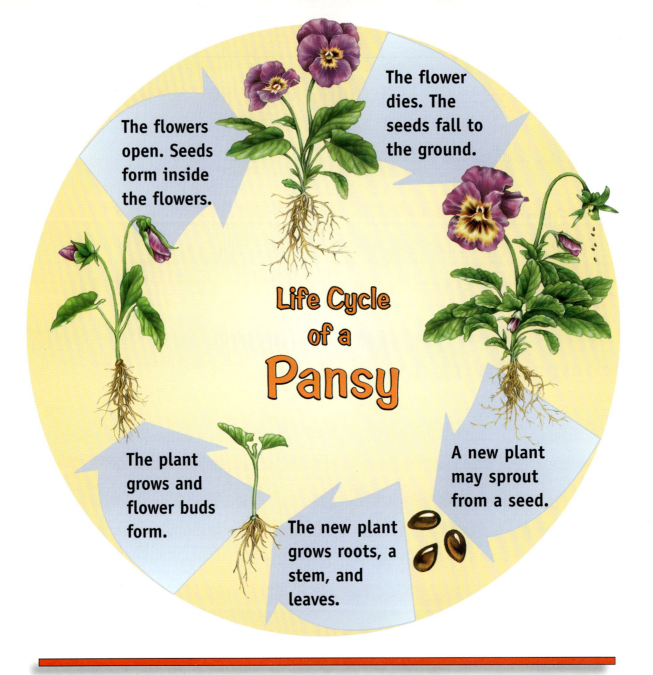

The Life Cycle of a Plant

All plants have life cycles. Most plants begin life as a **seed**. Some seeds form in **flowers**. Other seeds form in **cones**. Seeds grow into young plants and then into adult plants. Adult plants make seeds that can grow into new plants. An adult plant may die after dropping its seeds. The life cycle goes on.

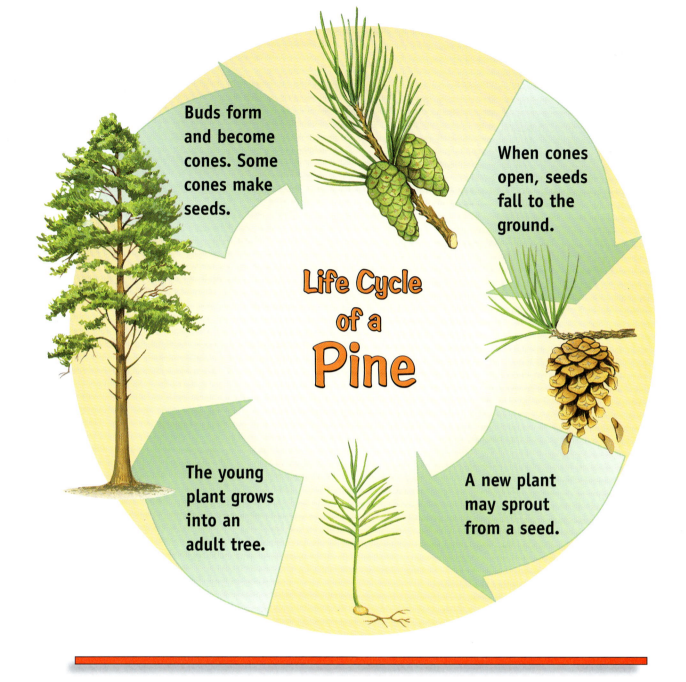

Some plants have short **life spans**—the time between birth and death. They begin to grow in spring and die before winter. Other plants have long life spans. The giant sequoia can live for hundreds or even thousands of years. The bristlecone pine tree, found in northern California, is almost five thousand years old.

Reading Check **Tell** about the stages in the life cycle of a plant.

LESSON 6: Where do some plants form seeds?

Activity
Examining Flowers and Fruits

What You Need

- goggles
- gloves
- lily flower
- hand lens
- fruits
- white paper
- Science Notebook

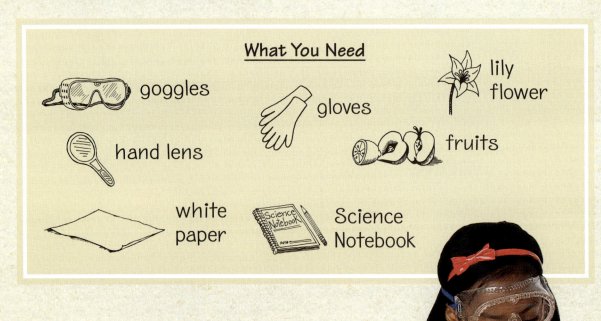

1 **Look at** a flower. **Draw a picture** of what you see.

Internet Field Trip

Visit **www.eduplace.com** to find out how plants make new plants.

❷ Shake the flower over a sheet of paper. Use a hand lens to **observe** the paper. **Record** what you see.

❸ **Talk with your group** about where the powder came from. **Record** what you **observed**.

❹ Carefully pull the petals apart. **Look at** the inside of the flower. **Talk with your group** about where the seeds might form. **Record** your ideas.

❺ **Observe** the insides of some fruits. **Record** what you see.

Think! How are flowers and fruits alike?

Flowers and Fruits

Seeds form inside the flowers of many adult plants. **Pollen**, a powdery material, is made by one part of the flower. Pollen is needed to make seeds form. There are tiny eggs inside some flowers. When pollen lands on the eggs, seeds may start to form. What happens to the flower after the seeds form?

Look at the large pictures of the apple-tree branch and the squash plant. Both plants have colorful flowers.

Now look at the small pictures. The flowers look different. After seeds form inside a flower, the flower begins to dry up. As the flower dies, the area around the seeds gets bigger. A **fruit** begins to form around the seeds. How will these plants change as they grow? Turn the page to find out.

The fruits are ready to eat. You may think a squash is a vegetable. But, like an apple, it is a fruit that forms around the seeds. Many foods you eat have seeds inside. All of these foods are fruits.

The seeds from the fruits can grow into new plants. The new plants inherit many traits from their parent plants. What traits do you think the young plants will inherit from the parent plants?

The new plants may have the same flower color and shape. They may grow to be the same size. They may live the same length of time. The new plants will grow the same kind of fruit. The new apple tree will grow apples. The new squash plant will grow squashes. The life cycle will go on.

Reading Check **Draw a picture** that shows where you might find seeds in some plants.

Lesson 7 How do new plants begin to grow?

Activity
Examining a Seed

What You Need

- goggles
- 6 lima beans
- toothpicks
- hand lens
- 2 wet paper towels
- masking tape
- 2 sealable plastic bags
- Science Notebook

1. Use a toothpick to open two lima bean seeds. **Look at** the inside of the seeds. **Draw** what you see.

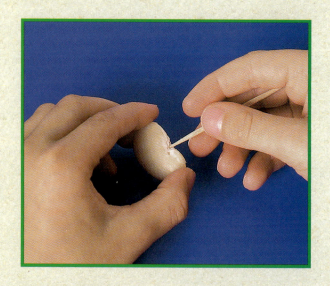

LIFE CYCLES

2. Place a paper towel in each bag. Place the four seed halves in one bag. Place four whole beans in the other bag. Seal the bags and tape them to a wall.

3. **Look at** the seeds each day for three days. **Record** what you see.

4. *Using Math* On the third day, remove a whole seed. Use a toothpick to open it. **Look at** the inside and **record** what you see.

5. Repeat steps 3–4 until you have opened all the whole seeds.

Think! Which grows better—the half seed or the whole seed? Why do you think so?

LESSON 7 ACTIVITY   A33

A Seed Is a Beginning

Different plants have different kinds of seeds. Seeds come in many sizes, shapes, and colors. All seeds need air, water, and sunlight to grow.

A tiny plant grows inside a seed. A seed is protected like an egg by a kind of shell. A seed's outside shell is called a **seed coat**.

Carrot

Avocado

Pumpkin

Seeds grow better when they have room to grow. Some seeds are carried away from their parent plants by wind or water. Animals also help move seeds. Sometimes seeds stick to an animal's fur. Some animals, such as birds and squirrels, eat fruits and carry seeds to a new location.

Reading Check **Write a story** about a seed that grows into a new plant.

Lesson 8
What things can affect how plants grow?

Activity
Observing Growing Plants

What You Need

 goggles

 2 seedlings in cups

 piece of plastic wrap

 shoebox with lid

 masking tape

 Science Notebook

1 Place one seedling in a shoebox away from the hole. Put the lid on the box. Don't let the plant touch the lid.

A36 LIFE CYCLES

❷ Place the plastic wrap over the other seedling. Gently fit the seedling through the hole in the wrap. Tape the wrap to the cup.

❸ Turn the cup upside down. Tape it to the bottom of a shelf or desk.

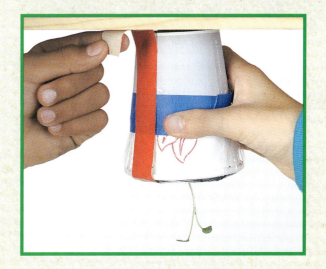

❹ **Predict** what the seedlings will look like in three days. **Record** your prediction.

❺ After three days, look at the seedlings. **Record** what you see.

Think! What caused the seedlings to change?

How Plants Adapt

Plants can change to **adapt** to where they live. Plants need light and water to make food. So they quickly grow toward both light and water.

A plant's stem grows toward light. If light comes from one side, the stem bends toward the light. This lets the plant get as much light as possible.

Roots and stems respond to the force of **gravity**. It is the force that pulls things toward the earth. The roots of plants grow down. They are growing toward the pull of gravity. This lets roots reach the water and minerals in soil. A plant needs both water and minerals to grow. Stems grow away from the pull of gravity. They grow up. If a seed is planted upside down, the roots will grow down and the stem will grow up.

Things in nature may affect a plant. Sometimes a plant can adapt to keep growing. Sometimes a plant may stop growing.

◀ The mimosa plant closes its leaves when it is touched. It is protecting itself from danger.

Cold wind blows hard on one side of this tree. Branches keep growing on the warm side of the trunk. ▶

◀ The flower on this plant was hurt by frost. It may not make seeds.

In autumn there is less sunlight and less water. To keep living, some kinds of trees take a rest from growing. These trees stop making food so the leaves are no longer green. The colorful leaves fall to the ground. The trees live on stored food and water. When there is more sunlight, the trees will grow again.

✔️ **Reading Check** **Tell** about three things that affect how plants grow.

LESSON 9: How are living things of one kind different?

Activity
Comparing Fruits

What You Need

 fresh fruits

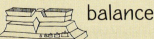 balance

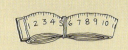 tape measure

 Science Notebook

1. **Look at** two of the same kind of fruit. **Record** how each one looks.

2. **Measure** the length of the two fruits. **Record** your measurements.

A42 LIFE CYCLES

❸ Use the balance to **measure** the mass of each fruit. **Record** your measurements.

❹ Repeat steps 1–3 for each kind of fruit.

Think! How are fruits of the same kind different?

Find Out More!

CD-ROM

Use **Science Blaster**™ **Jr.** Visit the Size-O-Meter to see a California redwood tree grow. Then compare it to other trees.

The Same, but Not the Same

Many living things of the same kind look alike. But in some ways they can look very different. The plants in the pictures are all the same kind. How are they alike?

The leaves of the plants are alike. Each of these plants looks like its parents. Seeds from these plants will grow new plants of the same kind.

How are these plants different? The flowers of the plants are different. The colors of each flower are different. Some flowers have petals that are pointed. Other flowers have petals that are rounded. Some of the petals are wide. Other petals are narrow.

Think about the children in your classroom. How are your classmates like you? How are your classmates different from you?

Look at the picture of the fruits and vegetables. They are sorted by kind. What differences can you see among foods of the same kind?

Look at the color, shape, size, and texture of each kind of food. How could you sort them differently?

Using Math

Sort the foods into groups that are alike in two ways. Name each group. One group could be round and red foods. Record your groups in a chart like the one shown.

Sorting Foods			
Round and red			

✓ **Reading Check** **Tell** how living things of one kind can be different.

Lesson 10: What things can affect a life cycle?

Activity

Washing Away the Soil

What You Need

- pan with soil and seeds in it
- pan with soil and plants in it
- towel
- books
- goggles
- watering can with water
- Science Notebook

1. Make a hill by putting books under one end of a pan with soil and seeds in it.

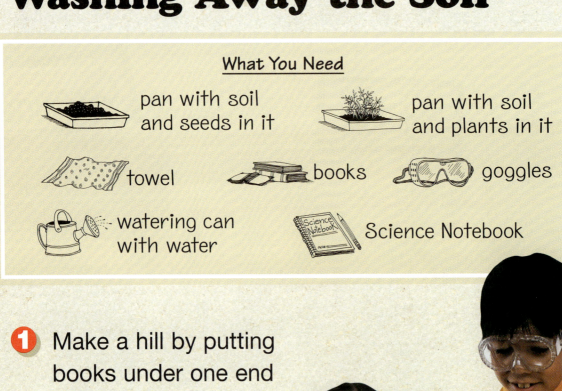

❷ Place a towel under the lower end of the pan. Pour water down the hill. **Record** what happens.

❸ Put books under one end of a pan with soil and plants in it.

❹ Repeat step 2.

Think! **How can water going down a hill affect a life cycle?**

Find Out More!

What other things can affect a life cycle? Make a plan to find out. Share your findings with your classmates.

Good or Bad?

Many events in nature can affect life cycles. A flood can kill plants by giving them too much water. It can kill animals, too, if they cannot escape to dry land.

Too little water can also affect living things. Plants need water to grow. If the plants cannot grow, the animals might not get enough food.

Forest fires can harm some living things but they can also help. Some kinds of trees need fire to make new trees. Heat from a fire opens the cones, and the seeds drop to the ground. Other plants are destroyed by the fire. The seeds have the space they need to grow into new trees. The life cycle goes on.

> ✓ **Reading Check** **Make a list** of things that affect plant and animal life cycles.

UNIT REVIEW

Word Power

If you need help, turn to the pages shown in blue.

Match a word with a picture. (A24–A25) (A28–A29)

    cone   fruit   seed

1.
2.
3.

Write the letter of the correct words.

4. Seeds grow in the _____ of many plants. (A24–A25)
   - a. pollen
   - b. flowers
   - c. roots
   - d. stems

5. A powdery material called _____ is needed for seeds to grow. (A28–A29)
   - a. cones
   - b. fruit
   - c. flowers
   - d. pollen

6. When plants change to live in a place, they _____. (A38–A39)
   - a. adapt
   - b. hatch
   - c. inherit
   - d. learn

7. Roots grow toward the pull of _____. (A38–A39)
   - a. fruit
   - b. eggs
   - c. gravity
   - d. seeds

8. The time between birth and death is called a _____. (A24–A25)
   - a. stage
   - b. life cycle
   - c. adult
   - d. life span

9. A seed's outer shell is called a _____. (A34–A35)
   - a. flower
   - b. seed coat
   - c. baby
   - d. life cycle

10. The ordered changes in the life of a plant or animal is called a _____. (A3–A4)
    - a. cones
    - b. life cycle
    - c. gravity
    - d. life span

Using Science Ideas

Tell about the life cycle of these young pine trees. What will affect how they grow?

Writing in Science

Choose a favorite plant or animal. Draw pictures to show the stages of its life cycle. Write a sentence to go with each stage. Then write a sentence that describes all the stages of the life cycle.

UNIT A

Sequence

These sentences tell about the stages in the life cycle of a frog. Write the sentences in the correct order. Then tell what will happen next to keep the cycle going.

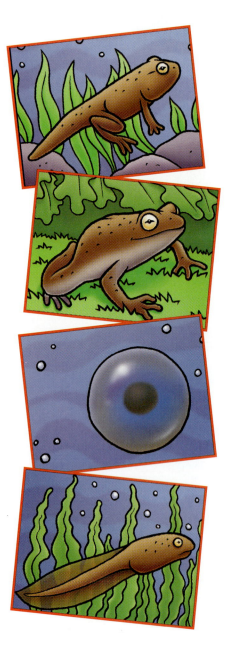

◀ As the tadpole grows, its legs form. The tail gets shorter.

◀ A frog has no tail. It has lungs to help it breathe on land.

◀ An egg lives in the water. If you touch it, it feels like jelly.

◀ A tadpole hatches from the egg. It has no legs and breathes using gills.

Using MATH SKILLS

 Make a Bar Graph

Michael wants to plant a garden. His grandmother gave him a bag of seeds. He made a chart to show how many of each kind of seed he has.

Kinds of Seeds		
Seed	Tally	Total
Bean	𝍷𝍷 ||	7
Pumpkin	𝍷𝍷 ||||	9
Corn	𝍷𝍷 𝍷𝍷	10
Watermelon	𝍷𝍷		6

Make a bar graph like the one shown below. Color one box for each kind of seed.

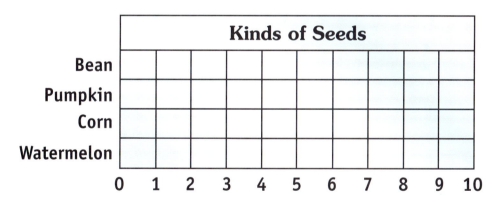

Use the graph to answer each question.

1. Which kind of seed is there the most of?
2. How many more corn seeds does Michael have than watermelon seeds?
3. How many bean and pumpkin seeds does Michael have altogether?
4. Michael wants the same number of bean and corn seeds. How many more bean seeds does he need?

Energy and Motion

Themes: Constancy and Change; Scale

LESSON 1 How does light move?
- **Activity** Observing the Path of Light B2
- **Resource** Light on the Move B4

LESSON 2 What things let light pass through?
- **Activity** Observing Light as It Strikes Objects. . B8
- **Resource** Can You See the Light? B10

LESSON 3 How do lenses change light?
- **Activity** Exploring Lenses. B14
- **Resource** Light Through Lenses B16

LESSON 4 How do you know when something moves?
- **Activity** Measuring Motion B18
- **Resource** Things in Motion. B20

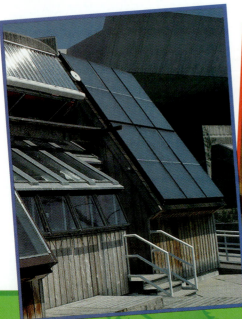

Lesson 5 What causes changes in motion?
Activity   Exploring Pushes B22
Resource Forces and Motion B24

Checkpoint B28

Lesson 6 What does motion have to do with sound?
Activity   Observing Motion and Sound B30
Resource Wiggles and Waves B32

Lesson 7 How can sounds be different?
Activity   Experimenting With High and
           Low Sounds B34
Resource High and Low, Loud and Soft. B36

Lesson 8 How is heat made?
Activity   Exploring Motion and Heat B40
Resource Making Heat B42

Lesson 9 How can heat be used and saved?
Activity   Exploring Ways to Save Heat B44
Resource Using Natural Resources B46

Unit Review B48

Using Reading Skills B50

Using Math Skills B51

Lesson 1: How does light move?

Activity

Observing the Path of Light

What You Need

flashlight, construction paper, mirror, crayons, Science Notebook

1. Darken the room. Shine a flashlight across a sheet of paper.

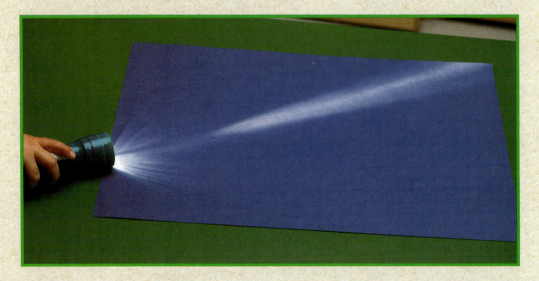

❷ Try to make the light curve or bend. **Record** what happens.

❸ Have a partner hold a mirror on the paper. Make the light hit the mirror. **Record** what you see.

❹ Change the position of the mirror. **Record** what you see.

Think! How can you change the direction of light?

Internet Field Trip

Visit **www.eduplace.com** to find out more about light.

Light on the Move

What fun it is to play flashlight tag! In this game, the person who is "it" shines a flashlight to tag another child. Think about how light moves. Where could you hide so that you don't get tagged? You might hide behind a tree. A tree blocks the path of **light**. The light cannot turn to go around the tree.

The light moves in straight lines until it hits an object. That's why you can point a flashlight at others and tag them with the light. You can't tag someone who is behind a tree.

How does light get from the porch light to the book? Light moves away from the bulb in all directions. Some of the light shines on the pages of the book. What are other objects light shines on?

Suppose you play flashlight tag again. This time, you are "it" and you have a partner. You want to tag a child behind a rock. How can you work together?

You can give your partner a mirror. Then you shine the flashlight at the mirror. The mirror **reflects** light. The light bounces off the mirror and moves in a new direction. Now the light shines behind the rock. The child is tagged!

ENERGY AND MOTION

A mirror reflects light. So do other objects. Light from the porch light hits the book. The pages of the book reflect some of the light. The light changes direction. The light keeps moving in straight lines to shine on the man's face. What else in the picture is reflecting light?

Reading Check Draw a picture to show how light can go around a corner.

LESSON 2: What things let light pass through?

Observing Light as It Strikes Objects

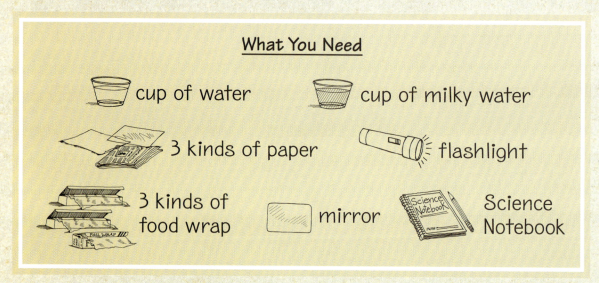

What You Need

- cup of water
- cup of milky water
- 3 kinds of paper
- flashlight
- 3 kinds of food wrap
- mirror
- Science Notebook

1. **Predict** whether all light, some light, or no light will pass through the objects. **Record** your predictions.

2 Darken the room. Shine a flashlight through a cup of clear water. **Record** what happens to the light.

3 Shine light through the other objects. **Record** what happens.

4 **Compare** your predictions with your observations.

Think! How are the objects that do not let light pass through them alike?

Can You See the Light?

Light passes through some objects. These objects are **transparent**. Some objects let a little light through. They are **translucent**. Other objects let no light pass through. These objects are **opaque**.

This picture has three coverings. Which one is opaque? Which is transparent? Which is translucent?

Think of other places you can see different coverings. Suppose you are helping to pack your lunch. You wrap your sandwich in a piece of wax paper. The sandwich looks blurred. That's because wax paper is translucent.

Suppose you put your sandwich in a wrap that is opaque. You might use aluminum foil or brown paper. What kind of wrap is transparent?

Look at the picture now. The coverings have been removed. You can see what was under the opaque and translucent coverings.

The transparent covering was clear. When it covered the picture, you could still see what was under it. What other things are transparent? Think of things you can see through. You might think of a window, clear water, or the air around you.

Suppose you are sitting at home at your desk. You hold up a ball in front of the lamp. The ball is opaque. It blocks the light and makes a **shadow**.

You are opaque, too. Stand in front of a light. Face away from the light. Look at your shadow. Wiggle your arms. How does your shadow change?

Reading Check **Make lists** of things that are transparent, translucent, and opaque.

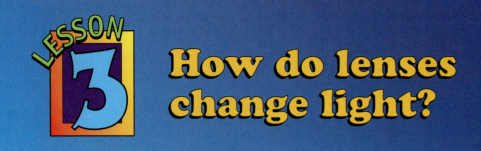

Lesson 3: How do lenses change light?

Activity
Exploring Lenses

What You Need

hand lens, newspaper, water, jar with lid, Science Notebook

1. Fill a jar with water. Put the lid on tightly.

2. Look through the jar at a piece of newspaper. **Observe** and **record** how the letters and words look.

❸ Move the jar away from you and back toward you. **Describe** how the letters seem to change.

❹ Repeat steps 2–3, using a hand lens. **Compare** what you see through the hand lens with what you saw through the jar of water.

Think! **How are a jar of water and a hand lens alike?**

Light Through Lenses

A container filled with water is curved and transparent. It is a kind of **lens**. When light strikes a lens, the light passes through. However, the light bends. The light moves in a new direction. Objects you see through a lens look different. Lenses can make objects look bigger or smaller.

There are many kinds of lenses in the picture. A pair of eyeglasses has two lenses. The hand lens has one. People and fish have a lens in each eye.

The water in the tank acts like a lens. It makes the handle of the net look bigger. Where else have you seen lenses change how something looks?

Reading Check **Write** about how lenses change the way you see an object.

LESSON 4: How do you know when something moves?

Activity
Measuring Motion

What You Need

- wax paper
- stack of books
- paper towel
- tape
- cardboard
- cup of water
- crayon
- tape measure
- dropper
- timer
- Science Notebook

1. Use a crayon to draw a starting line on the cardboard. Tape wax paper onto the cardboard.

ENERGY AND MOTION

❷ Make a pile of books about 10 centimeters high. Put the starting end of the cardboard on the books to make a ramp.

❸ Place a drop of water on the starting line. Time the drop for 4 seconds. Mark and **measure** how far the drop moved. **Record** your measurement.

❹ Use a paper towel to blot the water. Then repeat step 3. This time, **measure** how far the drop moves in 8 seconds. **Compare** the distances.

Measuring Motion	
Time	Distance
4 seconds	
8 seconds	

Think! What differences do you see in the two measurements? Why?

LESSON 4 ACTIVITY • B19

Things in Motion

A runner pushes off the starting blocks. A racecar zooms around a track. A flying disk sails through the air. A speed skater glides along an icy track. What do these things have in common?

They are all things in **motion**. When something is in motion, it changes its position.

What are some ways to measure motion? You can measure the distance something has traveled. Then you will know how far it has moved.

You can also use a stopwatch to measure how much time it took. A racecar can go more than three miles in one minute. That's a fast **speed**!

> ✅ **Reading Check Tell** how you know when something has moved.

Lesson 5
What causes changes in motion?

Activity
Exploring Pushes

What You Need

index card

marble

book

Science Notebook

① Make two folds along an index card. Place one end of the card on a book to make a ramp on the floor.

② Hold a marble at the top of the ramp. Let it go. **Observe** the direction it moves across the floor.

3 Roll the marble again. When it reaches the floor, try to change its direction by blowing on it. **Record** what happens.

> **Find Out More!**
>
> Experiment with pulls. Use a steel ball and a magnet. How can you change the motion of the ball without touching it?

4 Roll the marble again. This time, try to make it speed up by blowing on it. Then try to make it slow down. **Record** what you do and what happens.

Think! How did you use pushes to change the motion of the marble?

LESSON 5 ACTIVITY B23

Forces and Motion

Pushes and pulls are **forces**. Forces can change how fast an object is moving. This skater is using forces to speed up and slow down. To speed up, the skater pushes harder with one foot and then with the other. To stop, she drags the brake on the back of her skate. Dragging pulls her to a stop.

Forces can also change the direction in which an object is moving. As the skater rolls along, she pushes against one skate. The pushing makes her turn. She keeps pushing until she changes direction.

Do you play baseball, soccer, or basketball? Then you know about balls in motion. Think about the ball in each sport. How do you use forces to make it move, speed up, slow down, or change direction?

You know how people use forces to move objects. In what other ways are forces made to move things?

◀ A tractor can pull heavy farm machinery.

Magnets pull on some metal objects. The force of a magnet can move an object without touching it. ▶

◀ A bulldozer makes it easier to push soil and rocks.

Sometimes it is hard to see where a push or pull is coming from. The earth pulls on everything near it. This pull is called the force of **gravity**.

The force of gravity pulls objects toward the center of the earth. This ballet dancer will come back down to the floor because of gravity.

> ✔ **Reading Check** **Draw a picture** of an object in motion. Tell how a force can change the motion.

UNIT B CHECKPOINT

Word Power

If you need help, turn to the pages shown in blue.

Match a word with a picture. (B10–B11)

transparent   translucent   opaque

1.   2.   3.

Use these words to fill in the blanks.

light   lens   forces
gravity   reflects

4. A _____ bends light as the light passes through. (B16–B17)

5. _____ moves in straight lines. (B4–B5)

6. A mirror _____ light. (B6–B7)

7. Pushes and pulls are _____ . (B24–B25)

8. The force of _____ pulls everything toward the earth. (B26–B27)

Solving Science Problems

You want to cut out shapes to make dark shadows on the wall. Read the list of materials. Predict which ones you think will work best. Tell why you chose each one.

plastic wrap   tissue paper   wood
wax paper   cardboard   paper bag
aluminum foil   paper napkin

People Using Science

Lighting Technician

Lighting technicians use lights on stage for special effects. Red lights can look like fire. Flashing lights can look like lightning. Yellow lights can look like sunshine.

This lighting technician keeps track of which lights to use in each scene of a play. Why is it important to know which lights to use?

Using Math: Comparing Numbers

Compare the speeds of the animals in the pictures. Then answer the questions.

1. Which animal moves faster than a jack rabbit?

2. Is a human faster or slower than a kangaroo?

3. What might happen if an elephant and a human were in a race?

4. List the animals in order from slowest to fastest.

Lesson 6: What does motion have to do with sound?

Activity

Observing Motion and Sound

What You Need

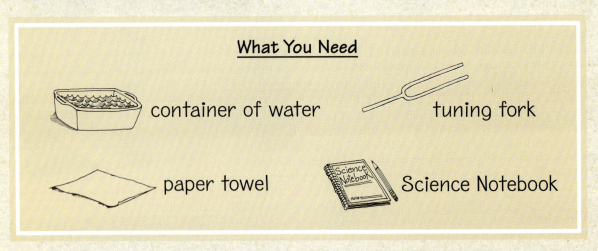

- container of water
- tuning fork
- paper towel
- Science Notebook

1 Hold a tuning fork near your ear. **Talk about** and **record** what you hear.

❷ Strike the tuning fork on the bottom of your shoe. Touch it with one finger. **Talk about** and **record** what you feel.

❸ Strike the tuning fork again. Hold it near your ear. **Talk about** and **record** what you hear.

❹ Strike the tuning fork again. Lower it slowly into some water. **Record** what you see on the surface of the water.

Think! What caused what you saw on the surface of the water?

Wiggles and Waves

Suppose you put a stick in water. Then you wiggle the stick back and forth quickly. This kind of motion is called a **vibration**.

Look at the picture. The stick makes the water move. **Waves** form and move away from the stick. You can see the waves on the surface of the water.

Waves can move through air, too. Suppose you pluck a harp string. It vibrates back and forth. It makes waves in the air around it. The waves spread out through the air. You cannot see these waves. However, you can hear them. Vibrations that make waves you hear are called **sound**.

> ✓ **Reading Check** **Tell** about waves that you can see and waves that you can't see.

Lesson 7 How can sounds be different?

Activity
Experimenting With High and Low Sounds

What You Need

paper cup   rubber band   goggles

Science Notebook

① Stretch a rubber band over the opening of a cup.

ENERGY AND MOTION

❷ Hold the cup near your ear. Gently pluck the rubber band. Listen to the sound. **Record** what you hear.

❸ Squeeze the cup to change the shape of the opening. **Predict** what you will hear. Then repeat step 2.

Think! How did the sounds you made compare?

Find Out More!

CD-ROM

Use **Science Blaster Jr.** to find out more about sound. Create and play songs. Listen to them and see how the waves change.

High and Low, Loud and Soft

Vibrations can be slow. Vibrations can be fast. Slow vibrations make a low sound. A gong makes a low sound.

Fast vibrations make a high sound. Finger cymbals vibrate faster than a gong. They make a high sound. **Pitch** is how high or how low a sound is.

Sounds can be soft. Sounds can be loud. The ticking of a clock is a very soft sound. A clock's alarm is a very loud sound.

The loudness of a sound is called its **volume**. Radios and televisions have volume controls. You use these controls to make the sounds that you hear louder or softer. On what other objects might you change the volume of a sound?

These sound makers have been put in order by their volume. The softest sound is a baby breathing. The sound a vacuum cleaner makes is louder than the sound of a ringing telephone. Two girls talking is a softer sound than a rock band playing.

The loudest sound is a jet taking off. Sounds as loud as the engine of a jet can hurt people's ears. That is why the worker is wearing ear protection.

Soft

Using Math

Answer these questions about the order of the pictures. The softest sound is first.

1. Which sound is third?
2. Which sound is fifth?
3. Which sound is second?
4. Is the fourth sound or the sixth sound louder?

!Loud

✓ **Reading Check** **Write** about some sound makers you know. Describe the pitch and volume of their sounds.

Lesson 8: How is heat made?

Activity

Exploring Motion and Heat

What You Need

2 pencils   goggles   Science Notebook

1. Hold two pencils to your cheeks. **Observe** how hot or cold they feel.

2. Rub one pencil against the other 20 times.

❸ Hold the pencils to your cheeks again. **Observe** and **record** how hot or cold they feel.

❹ Hold your hands to your cheeks. **Observe** how hot or cold they feel.

❺ **Predict** how your hands will feel when you rub them together 20 times. **Test** it out. **Record** what happens.

Think! What did you do to the pencils and your hands to make heat?

Internet Field Trip

Visit www.eduplace.com to find out more about heat.

Making Heat

There are many ways to make heat. How many can you name in the picture?

Objects in motion can make **heat**. That is why people rub their arms with their hands to warm up. Bicycle brakes get hot when they rub against the wheel. Whenever two surfaces rub together, heat is made.

Burning things also make heat. Burning wood in a campfire makes a lot of heat. Burning charcoal in a grill also makes a lot of heat.

Light from the sun makes heat, too. In the picture the sun is making the sand on the beach very hot. What else is being warmed by the sun?

Reading Check **Draw a picture** of three different ways to make heat.

LESSON 9: How can heat be used and saved?

Activity
Exploring Ways to Save Heat

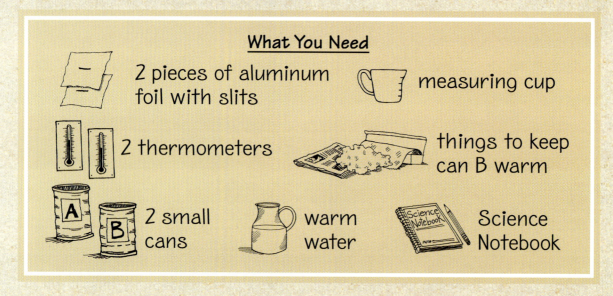

What You Need
- 2 pieces of aluminum foil with slits
- measuring cup
- 2 thermometers
- things to keep can B warm
- 2 small cans
- warm water
- Science Notebook

① **Make a plan** to keep a can of water warm. **Record** your plan.

② Pour 1 cup of warm water into can A and can B. Cover the cans with foil pieces. Put a thermometer through the slit into the water in each can.

B44 ENERGY AND MOTION

3 Wait 1 minute. **Measure** and **record** the water temperature in each can. Use can B to **test your plan**.

4 Wait 10 minutes. **Measure** and **record** the water temperature in each can.

Find Out More!

How do people use heat? Make a plan to find out. Try out your plan. Report what you find.

Exploring Ways to Save Heat		
	Can A	Can B
Temperature after 1 minute		
Temperature after 10 minutes		

Think! How did your plan keep the water in can B warm?

LESSON 9 ACTIVITY

Using Natural Resources

The earth includes many living and nonliving things. Trees and fish are some living things. Rocks, soil, water, and air are nonliving things. All of these things are used by people. They are **natural resources**.

Some natural resources are used for food. Some are used for shelter. Some are used to make heat.

People use heat to cook food and warm their homes. Gas, oil, coal, and wood are some of the natural resources used to make heat. People can save these natural resources by using only as much as they need. What other natural resources do people use for heat?

Reading Check Write a story about people who use and save heat from natural resources.

UNIT B UNIT REVIEW

Word Power

If you need help, turn to the pages shown in blue.

Match a word with a picture. (B13, B16, B32)

shadow   lens   waves

1.   2.   3.

Write the letter of the correct word.

4. A ball rolling is an object in _____. (B20–B21)
   a. motion   b. sound   c. pitch   d. volume

5. How fast something moves is its _____. (B20–B21)
   a. gravity   b. shadow   c. speed   d. vibration

6. A _____ is a back-and-forth motion. (B32–B33)
   a. light   b. volume   c. shadow   d. vibration

7. The _____ of an instrument is how high or low it sounds. (B36–B37)
   a. wave   b. pitch   c. volume   d. speed

8. The loudness of a sound is its _____. (B36–B37)
   a. wave   b. pitch   c. volume   d. speed

9. Rubbing two objects together will make _____. (B42–B43)
   a. gravity   b. sound   c. heat   d. pitch

10. We use some of the earth's _____ to make heat. (B46–B47)
    a. motion   b. speed   c. gravity   d. natural resources

B48   ENERGY AND MOTION

Using Science Ideas

How many examples of motion can you find in this picture? List them.

Writing in Science

Besides being used to make heat, trees have many other uses. Make a list of the ways trees are used. Then list ways to save this natural resource.

UNIT B Using Reading Skills

Cause and Effect

Look at each picture and read the sentence that tells about it. Write or draw one effect for each action.

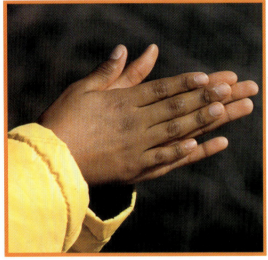
▲ Hope rubs her hands together.

▲ Amy pushes hard with her foot.

▲ A mirror is in the path of light.

▲ Sam turns the volume down on the radio.

Using MATH SKILLS

Use Data From a Picture

Use the picture to answer the questions.

1. Which ball moved the greatest distance?
2. Which ball moved the least distance?
3. How many meters did the red team's balls move altogether?
4. How many meters did the blue team's balls move altogether?
5. How much farther did ball 4 move than ball 2?

Earth's Materials

Themes: Systems; Models

LESSON 1 What kinds of soil cover the earth's land?
Activity   Examining Kinds of Soil C2
Resource   Looking at Soil C4

LESSON 2 What does soil contain?
Activity   Analyzing Soil C6
Resource   Looking Closer at Soil C8

LESSON 3 What happens to soil when water is added?
Activity   Examining Soil and Water C12
Resource   Water in Soil C14

LESSON 4 How do we use soil, plants, and water?
Activity   Exploring Uses of Plants and Water . C16
Resource   Using Soil, Plants, and Water C18

Checkpoint C22

Lesson 5 How large are rocks?
Activity   Examining Sizes of Rocks C24
Resource   Looking at Size C26

Lesson 6 What causes weathering and erosion?
Activity   Observing How Water Flows C28
Resource   Weathering and Erosion C30

Lesson 7 How can you compare different rocks and minerals?
Activity   Testing the Hardness of Rocks C34
Resource   Looking at Rocks and Minerals C36

Lesson 8 What can we learn from fossils?
Activity   Exploring Fossils C40
Resource   Learning About the Past C42

Lesson 9 How can rocks and minerals be grouped?
Activity   Looking at Rocks C46
Resource   Grouping Rocks and Minerals C48

Lesson 10 How do we use rocks and minerals?
Activity   Looking for Rocks C50
Resource   Living With Rocks and Minerals . . . C52

Unit Review C54

Using Reading Skills C56

Using Math Skills C57

C1

Lesson 1
What kinds of soil cover the earth's land?

Activity
Examining Kinds of Soil

What You Need

 goggles    topsoil   clay soil

 sandy soil   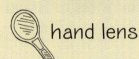 hand lens   Science Notebook

❶ Look at and touch three kinds of soil.

C2 EARTH'S MATERIALS

❷ **Look at** each kind of soil with a hand lens.

❸ **Record** what you see.

Think! How are these kinds of soil alike, and how are they different?

Looking at Soil

Soil covers much of the earth's land. Soil forms when **rock** breaks into tiny pieces.

Plants grow in soil. Look at the picture. You see grass, a tree, and flowers growing in the soil. You see the top layer of soil when you look at the ground. You don't see the layers under it.

In some places, the top layer of soil is dark and loose. This is called **topsoil**. Plants grow well in topsoil. Sometimes **clay soil** is under topsoil. Some places near oceans or lakes have **sandy soil**.

Every place on the earth has rock below it. Even oceans have rock under them.

Reading Check **Write** about the kinds of soil that cover the earth's land. What grows in soil?

Lesson 2: What does soil contain?

Activity
Analyzing Soil

What You Need

 goggles

 cup of soil

 hand lens

 2 large sheets of paper

 Science Notebook

1. Spread out soil on a sheet of paper. Use a hand lens to **look at** the soil.

EARTH'S MATERIALS

❷ Place things you find in the soil on another sheet of paper.

❸ **Group** things that are alike. **Draw** each group. Use two words to describe each group.

Using Math

Think! What kinds of things did you find in the soil?

Internet Field Trip

Visit **www.eduplace.com** to learn more about soil.

LESSON 2 ACTIVITY   C7

Looking Closer at Soil

Soil is made of many things. New soil is always being made. The things in the picture can become new parts of soil.

The logs and the leaves in the picture are not living now. They are **once-living things**. When they were living, they were parts of a tree.

A tree is a living thing. **Living things** need air, water, and food to stay alive. What things in the picture can help living things meet their needs?

A rock is a nonliving thing. **Nonliving things** do not need air, water, and food. Living things, nonliving things, and once-living things can be found in soil.

What kinds of things might you find under the log? Turn the page to find out.

The large log has been rolled away. What living things do you see where the log was? You see plants and tiny animals that live in soil. The hand lenses make the things in the soil look bigger than they are.

What nonliving things do you see? You see small pieces of rock.

Look through the hand lenses again. What are some once-living things that you see?

You see pieces of dry leaves and twigs. These things were once parts of a tree. They no longer need air, water, and food because they are not living.

Think about a time when you looked under a rock or a log. What kinds of things did you find? Which things were living, nonliving, and once-living?

✓ **Reading Check** **Draw a picture** of some things you might find in soil.

Lesson 3 What happens to soil when water is added?

Activity
Examining Soil and Water

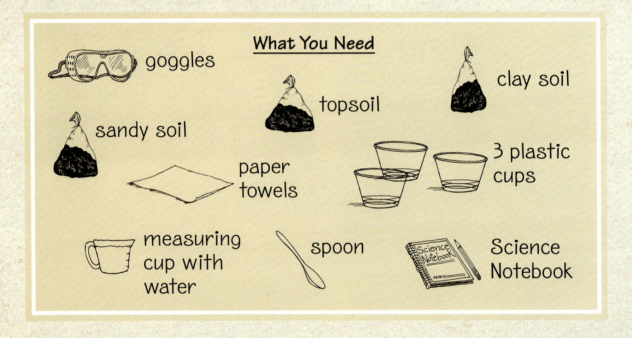

What You Need

goggles, sandy soil, topsoil, clay soil, paper towels, 3 plastic cups, measuring cup with water, spoon, Science Notebook

1. Place paper towels under three plastic cups.

2. Fill half of cup 1 with topsoil. Fill half of cup 2 with clay soil. Fill half of cup 3 with sandy soil.

EARTH'S MATERIALS

❸ **Measure** $\frac{1}{4}$ cup of water. Pour it onto the topsoil. **Record** what you see.

❹ Repeat step 3 for the clay soil and the sandy soil. **Record** what you see each time.

Think! **What happened to the water in each cup? Why did this happen?**

Find Out More!

How could you find out the best amount of water to give a plant growing in topsoil? List the steps you would take to find an answer. Use the list and tell what you find.

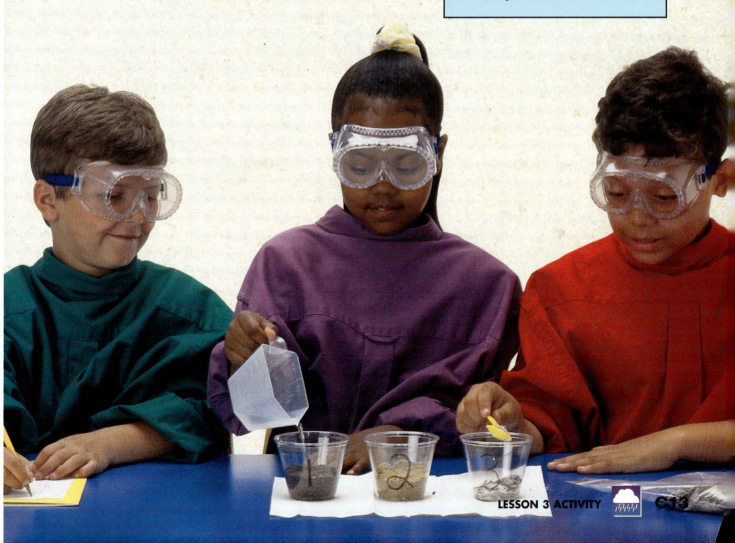

Water in Soil

Soil is made of tiny rocks and once-living things. There are many little air spaces in soil. Topsoil and sandy soil have more air spaces than clay soil has. When it rains, water soaks into these spaces. If there is more water than the spaces in the soil can hold, **puddles** may form.

Over time, some water from the puddles evaporates, or disappears into the air. Water from the puddles may also slowly absorb, or soak, into the soil.

The water in the soil is used by living things. Look at the pictures. What living things use the water that is in the soil?

Reading Check **Tell** what happens to soil after it rains. Why do puddles form?

Lesson 4: How do we use soil, plants, and water?

Activity
Exploring Uses of Plants and Water

What You Need

discarded magazines

glue

scissors

Science Notebook

1. **Look for** pictures in magazines that show how people use plants and water.

❷ Cut out the pictures. **Sort** them into groups to show different uses.

❸ **Record** the uses you find.

Think! In what ways do people use plants and water?

Find Out More!
CD-ROM

Visit the Engineering Room in **Science Blaster Jr.** to learn more about sorting plants.

LESSON 4 ACTIVITY   C17

Using Soil, Plants, and Water

Most things that people need to live come from the earth. People need food, water, and air to live. They also need a **shelter**, or a home. Homes protect people from danger and from bad weather.

Air is all around for people to use. But people need to find the other things they need to live.

Look at the picture. How has the family that lives here found what they need?

The family has built a house from trees. They also use wood from trees to heat their house. Trees have even been used to make the paper in the books and magazines they read.

The family grows vegetables such as lettuce to eat. They also grow fruits such as apples.

People use many things from the earth. Look at the pictures.

Plants

Cotton grows in warm places. People use it for clothing, curtains, and other things.

Potatoes grow underground. They are one of the many plants that people eat.

Soil

Clay is used to make dishes and vases. It is formed into shapes and then dried and heated.

Water

People use water to drink. They also use it for fun.

Reading Check **Make a list** of the ways you use soil, plants, and water.

LESSON 4 RESOURCE   C21

UNIT C CHECKPOINT

Word Power

If you need help, turn to the pages shown in blue.

Match the words with a picture. (C4, C9, C18)

living things   rocks   shelter

1.
2.
3.

Use these words to fill in the blanks.

topsoil   once-living   puddles

4. When there is more water than soil can hold, _____ may form. (C14–C15)

5. A top layer of dark, loose soil is called _____. (C4–C5)

6. Fallen leaves are _____ things. (C8–C9)

Solving Science Problems

Look at the picture. Explain what the problem is. Then tell how you could help to solve the problem.

People Using Science

Ecologist

Ecologists study living things and the places where they live. Ecologists might study life underwater, in a rain forest, or in the air. They might study soil to find out what kinds of plants grow in it.

How can knowing what an ecologist learns about soil and plants help people?

Make a Tally Chart

Make a tally chart like the one below. Then use the pictures to complete the chart.

Kinds of Things

Thing	Tally	Total
Living		
Nonliving		
Once-living		

LESSON 5 — How large are rocks?

Activity
Examining Sizes of Rocks

What You Need

goggles, rocks, sand, hand lens, Science Notebook

1. Spread rocks and sand on a table.

2. **Look at** each rock with a hand lens. **Draw** what you see.

❸ **Look at** the sand with a hand lens.
Draw what you see.

Think! How are the rocks and the sand alike, and how are they different?

Find Out More!

How many pieces of rock are in a pinch of sand? Make a plan to find an answer. What tools will you need? Compare your findings with those of other groups.

Looking at Size

Rocks come in many sizes. Very big rocks are called **boulders**.

The picture shows rocks of different sizes. The very big rock in the front is a boulder. It is the biggest rock in the picture. The rocks in the water are smaller than the boulder.

After a long time, moving water and wind wear away rocks. They make the rocks smaller. **Sand** is made up of tiny pieces of broken rock.

What might you find on the bottom of a river? Look at the small picture. It shows small rocks and sand at the bottom of a river.

✔ **Reading Check** **Tell** about rocks in a river. Use the words big, small, sand, and boulder.

Lesson 6 What causes weathering and erosion?

Activity

Observing How Water Flows

What You Need

goggles, wet sand, pan, button, measuring cup of water, Science Notebook

1. Use wet sand to make a small hill in a pan.

C28 EARTH'S MATERIALS

❷ Put a button in a place where you **predict** water will flow.

❸ **Measure** one cup of water. Slowly pour the water from the measuring cup onto the top of the hill.

Using Math

❹ **Watch** where the water flows. **Observe** what happens to the sand.

❺ **Record** what you see. **Tell** whether your prediction matched your results.

Think! Where did the water flow? What happened to the sand?

Weathering and Erosion

The earth is always changing. Wind, water, and other things break rocks. This is called **weathering**.

Water gets into the tiny cracks in rocks. When the water freezes, it swells. After many years, this makes rocks break. You can see where a crack in the face carved from rock has been repaired.

Wind can weather rocks, too. Look at the picture in the middle. Rain and wind wore away parts of the rocks. It may take millions of years for all the rock to wear away.

Even plants can break up rock. Look at the picture on the right. The tree roots grew into the rock. They caused the rock to break. The rock will break into smaller and smaller pieces as the roots grow.

Sometimes wind and water move soil and rocks. When this happens, it is called **erosion**.

Moving water is very strong. It is strong enough to cut a path through rocks. The picture below shows water moving downhill in a small river called a stream. The water is moving fast. It wears away some rocks. It carries other rocks downhill as it moves. The water is causing the erosion of the rocks.

Both wind and water can cause erosion in soil. Wind blows away topsoil, and rain carries topsoil downhill.

The picture shows erosion where there are not many roots to hold the soil back. Roots help hold soil in place. People can prevent soil erosion by planting trees, grass, and other plants.

Reading Check Work with a partner to **act out** how rock is changed by weathering and erosion.

Lesson 7 — How can you compare different rocks and minerals?

Activity
Testing the Hardness of Rocks

What You Need

goggles

rocks

tile

Science Notebook

① Spread rocks on a table.

❷ Squeeze each rock in your hand. **Record** how each rock feels.

❸ Use your fingernail to scratch each rock. **Record** what you **observe**.

❹ Then scratch a tile with each rock. **Record** what you **observe**.

Testing Hardness of Rocks			
Rock 1			

❺ **Compare** the rocks.

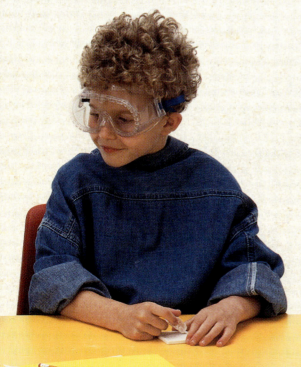

Think! Which rocks are the hardest? Tell how you know.

Looking at Rocks and Minerals

Minerals are materials that are formed in the earth and water. They are nonliving things. Rocks are made from one or more minerals.

There are different ways of finding out what rocks and minerals are made of. One way is to look at the **texture**, or how a rock or mineral feels.

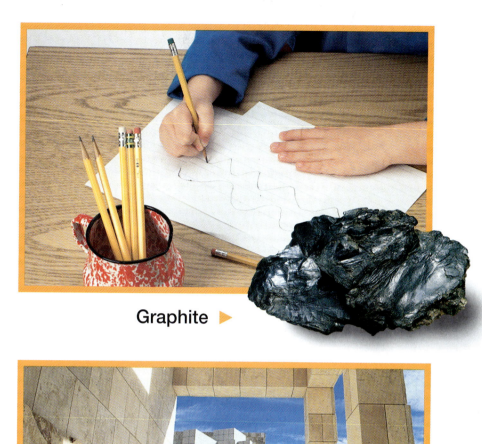

◀ Graphite

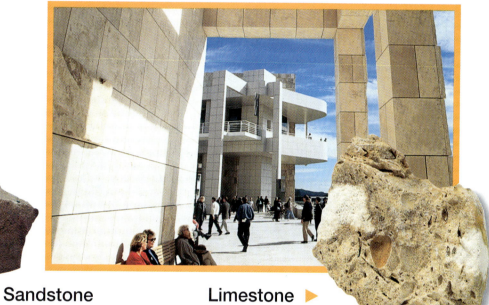

◀ Sandstone   Limestone ▶

The artist is using a rock called sandstone. Sandstone has a sandy texture. He grinds up the rock to make fine sand. Then he uses it to make a picture.

Color also helps scientists know what rocks and minerals are made of. The graphite is a shiny gray mineral that is used in pencils.

You can tell that the rock in the building has many minerals in it. It has many colors.

Hardness is another way to tell what a mineral is made of. A hard mineral can **scratch**, or make a mark on, a softer one. A soft mineral can't scratch a hard one.

◀ Talc is the softest mineral. It is used to make powder.

Diamonds are the hardest minerals. They are used in jewelry. ▶

◀ Bauxite contains aluminum. Aluminum is used to make foil and baking pans.

Cinnabar is not very hard. It is used in thermometers. ▶

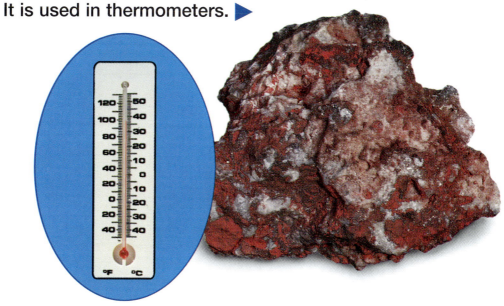

Using Math

Look at the table. The highest numbers show the hardest minerals.

Hardness of Minerals				
	Bauxite	Cinnabar	Diamond	Talc
Hardness	3	2	10	1

Use the table to answer the questions.

1. Which mineral is harder than bauxite?
2. Can cinnabar scratch bauxite? Tell how you know.
3. Put the minerals in order from softest to hardest.

Reading Check **Tell** how different rocks and minerals can be compared.

Lesson 8: What can we learn from fossils?

Activity
Exploring Fossils

What You Need

- goggles
- paper plate
- once-living objects
- 2 fossils
- hand lens
- dough
- Science Notebook

1 Use a hand lens to **observe** two fossils. **Draw** what you see.

EARTH'S MATERIALS

❷ **Talk about** what kinds of living things made these fossils. **Decide** if they were plants or animals.

❸ **Draw** how you think these plants or animals looked.

❹ Flatten some dough on a paper plate. Press an object into the dough and carefully remove it. This is a model fossil.

❺ **Compare** the model you made with the real fossils.

Think! Which fossil is more like the model you made? Tell why.

LESSON 8 ACTIVITY C41

Learning About the Past

Fossils are the remains or traces of once-living things. The parts of once-living things that change to rock are called **fossil remains**. The traces or outlines of once-living things in rocks are called **trace fossils**.

It takes millions of years for fossils to form. Fossils help us know what life was like long ago.

The shape of a leaf in rock is also a trace fossil. The leaf rotted but its outline is still there. ▶

The picture on page C42 shows fossil remains of a dinosaur. When the dinosaur died, mud covered it. The soft parts of its body rotted. Millions of years passed. Slowly, the hard parts of its body changed to rock.

The pictures on this page show trace fossils. Millions of years ago, a dinosaur walked on soft mud. The dinosaur left footprints. Slowly, the mud changed into rock. The footprints show how a dinosaur moved.

▲ Scientists put together fossil remains to learn how big animals were.

When scientists look at the rings on fossil remains of trees, they can tell how long the trees were alive. ▶

EARTH'S MATERIALS

◀ Many fossils are found where there was water millions of years ago. Mud helped bury plants, animals, and their traces.

▲ Scientists work carefully when they dig out fossils. They label fossils to show what they are and where they were found.

Reading Check **Write** about ways in which fossils help us learn about the past.

LESSON 8 RESOURCE   C45

LESSON 9: How can rocks and minerals be grouped?

Activity
Looking at Rocks

What You Need

- goggles
- paper plates
- balance
- rocks
- Science Notebook

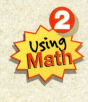

① Spread out rocks on a table. **Look at** and feel each rock.

② **Measure** the mass of each rock on a balance.

EARTH'S MATERIALS

❸ Decide how to **group** the rocks. Use two or more words to help you decide on groups.

❹ Put each group on a paper plate. **Draw** and label each group.

Think! How did you group the rocks?

Internet Field Trip
Visit **www.eduplace.com** to learn more about rocks and minerals.

Grouping Rocks and Minerals

You have learned a lot about rocks and minerals. You know that they come in many shapes and sizes. They have different colors. Some rocks and minerals are harder than others. You know that some rocks have fossil remains of plants or animals. Some rocks contain trace fossils.

Rocks and minerals have different textures. Some are smooth. Others are rough. Some rocks and minerals break into thin sheets. Others break into chunks. Some break into little pieces of sand.

Look at the rocks in the picture. What groups could you make?

Reading Check Make a group of rocks from the picture. **Write** about how the rocks are alike.

LESSON 10: How do we use rocks and minerals?

Activity

Looking for Rocks

What You Need

 crayons

 Science Notebook

1. **Think** about rocks and minerals. **Predict** where you will find them around your school.

2. Take a walk around the inside and outside of your school. Look for rocks and minerals.

3. **Draw** pictures of the rocks and minerals you see. **Write** or **tell** about where you see them.

EARTH'S MATERIALS

4. **Compare** what you saw with your predictions.

Think! Why are rocks and minerals important in people's lives?

LESSON 10 ACTIVITY

Living With Rocks and Minerals

Imagine what life would be like with no rocks and minerals. Look at the pictures. How would they be different if there were no rocks and minerals?

The skyscrapers are made of rock, steel, and glass. Steel is made from iron, which is a mineral. Glass is made from rocks and minerals.

The truck and the bicycles are made of metals. Metals come from rocks. The grass, and trees are growing in soil. Soil is made of rock.

The silverware is made of metal. The dishes are made from clay. The food even has minerals such as iron. People can't live without rocks and minerals.

Reading Check Look at the pictures. **Tell** as many ways as you can how people use rocks and minerals.

Unit Review

Word Power

If you need help, turn to the pages shown in blue.

Match the words with a picture. (C26–C27, C42–C43)

    boulder   fossil remains   trace fossil

1.

2.

3.

Write the letter of the correct word.

4. Wind and moving water cause the _____ of rocks. (C30–C31)
   - **a.** shelter   **b.** puddles   **c.** growth   **d.** weathering

5. The _____ of a rock is how it feels. (C36–C37)
   - **a.** scratch   **b.** texture   **c.** shelter   **d.** clay soil

6. Hard rocks can _____ softer rocks. (C38–C39)
   - **a.** clay   **b.** topsoil   **c.** scratch   **d.** minerals

7. When water or wind moves soil, it is called _____. (C32–C33)
   - **a.** erosion   **b.** shelter   **c.** minerals   **d.** growth

8. Plants, animals, and people could not live without rocks and _____. (C36–C37)
   - **a.** fossil remains   **b.** sandy soil   **c.** minerals   **d.** weathering

Using Science Ideas

Look at the picture. List the living things you see. Next, list the once-living things you see. Then list the nonliving things you see.

Writing in Science

A space explorer has found a rock on the moon. You are a newspaper reporter. You need to get some facts about the moon rock. Make a list of questions to ask about the moon rock.

Unit C · Using Reading Skills

Compare and Contrast

Robert made a chart to compare two rocks in his collection. He thought about questions that would help him.

	Limestone	Sandstone
What is its color?	brown and white	tan
What is its texture?	rough	sandy
Does it contain fossil remains?	yes	no

Choose two rocks or minerals you have seen. Think about how they are alike and different. Make a chart to compare them the way Robert did.

Using MATH SKILLS

Make a Bar Graph

Look at the rocks and minerals in the picture. Make a bar graph to show the number of rocks and minerals of each color. Fill in one box for each rock or mineral of each color.

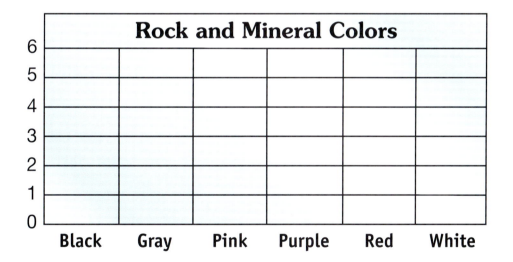

Use the graph to answer each question.

1. What is the color of the greatest number of these rocks and minerals?

2. How many more gray rocks and minerals are there than pink ones?

3. What is the total number of rocks and minerals?

UNIT D

What Makes Me Sick

Themes: Systems; Scale

LESSON 1 What are germs?
Activity   Making Clay Models D2
Resource   Looking at Germs. D4

LESSON 2 How does a sneeze spread germs?
Activity   Examining a Pretend Sneeze D6
Resource   Sneezing Spreads Germs D8

LESSON 3 What are other ways that germs are spread?
Activity   Examining How Germs Travel D10
Resource   Germs Everywhere D12

LESSON 4 How does your body protect you from germs?
Activity   Examining How Dust Collects. D16
Resource   Trapping Germs D18

Checkpoint. D20

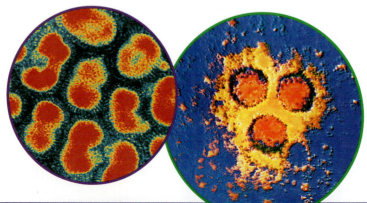

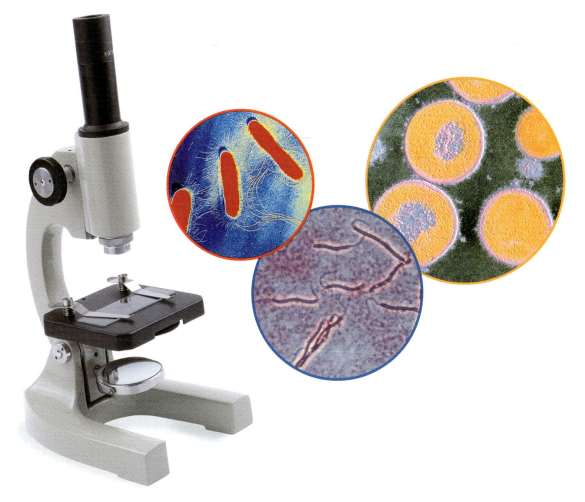

LESSON 5 How can you prevent the spread of germs?
Activity   Stopping Germs From Spreading .. D22
Resource   Protect Yourself D24

LESSON 6 How can you prevent sickness and injury?
Activity   Examining Health and Safety D28
Resource   Preventing Injury............... D30

LESSON 7 How can you stay healthy?
Activity   Exploring Healthful Activities D34
Resource   Staying Healthy D36

Unit Review............................ D38

Using Reading Skills D40

Using Math Skills D41

LESSON 1: What are germs?

Activity
Making Clay Models

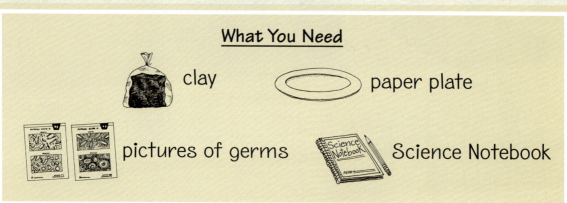

What You Need

clay   paper plate

pictures of germs   Science Notebook

❶ Study some microscope pictures of germs. **Look at** the shapes of the germs.

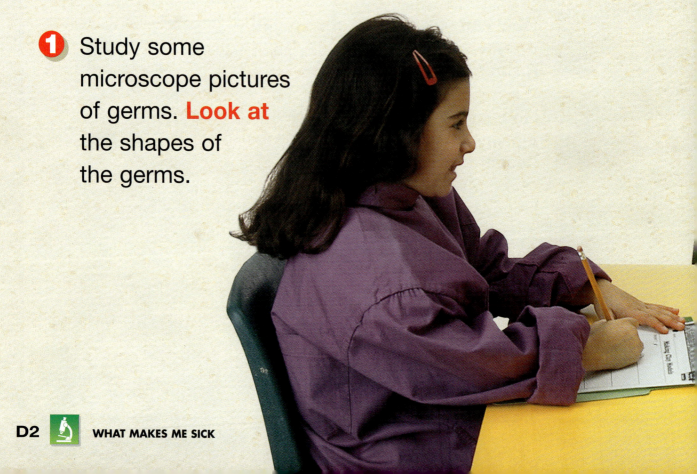

❷ Use small pieces of clay to **make models** of the different germs you see.

❸ **Draw** your models.

Find Out More!

CD-ROM

Visit the **Science Blaster™ Jr.** time line. Find out when the microscope was invented.

Think! How are your models like real germs? How are they different?

D3

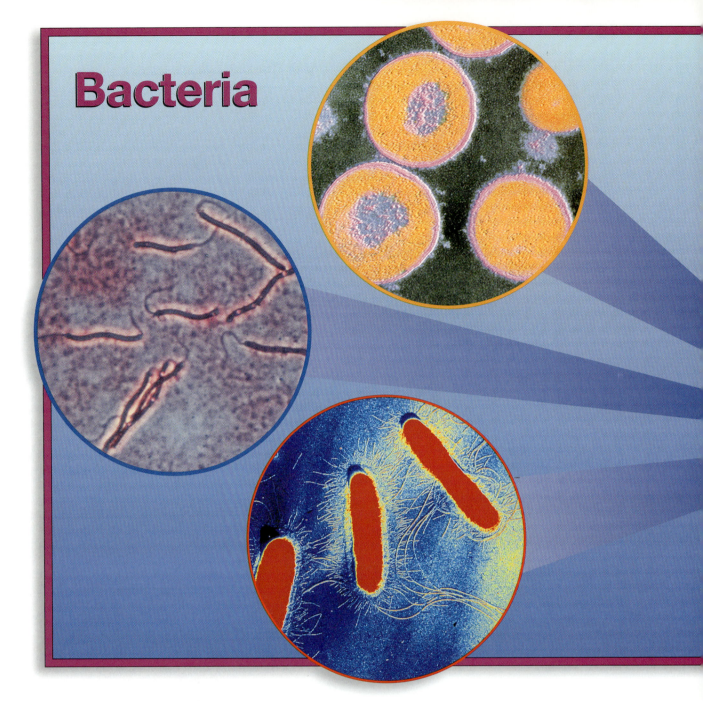

Looking at Germs

Germs can get inside your body. They can make you sick. Bacteria and viruses are two kinds of germs. Different germs cause different sicknesses.

Bacteria are very small living things. Bacteria cause some kinds of sore throats. If you do not brush your teeth, bacteria can cause tooth decay.

WHAT MAKES ME SICK

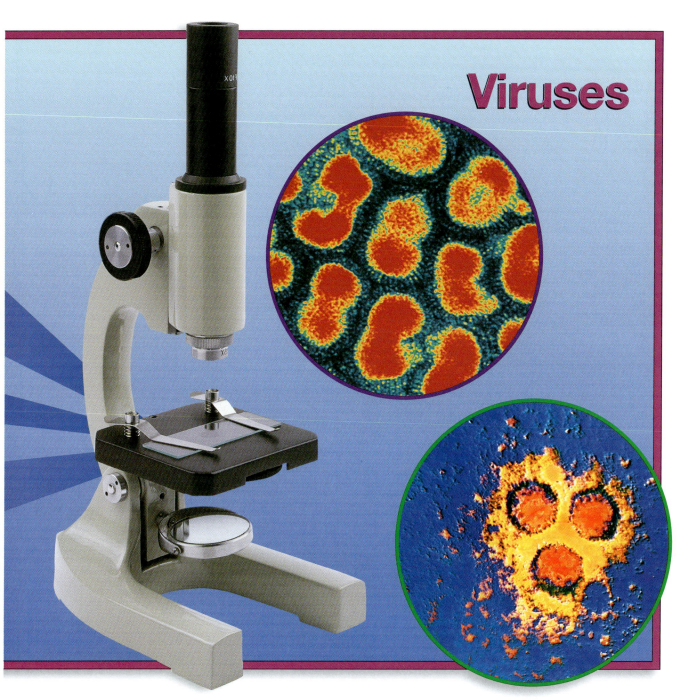

Viruses

Viruses grow inside living things. They cause colds and flu. Another virus causes chickenpox.

Germs are very small. A **microscope** helps you see things that are very small. The picture shows what some germs look like under a microscope. You need a very powerful microscope to see a virus.

Reading Check Tell about two kinds of germs and how they are alike and different.

LESSON 2
How does a sneeze spread germs?

Activity
Examining a Pretend Sneeze

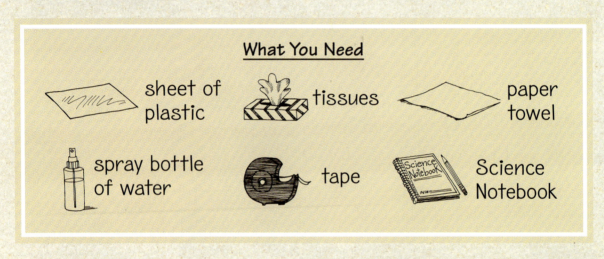

What You Need

- sheet of plastic
- tissues
- paper towel
- spray bottle of water
- tape
- Science Notebook

1. Tape a sheet of plastic to a wall. Spray water on the plastic. **Record** what you see.

2 Use a paper towel to dry the plastic.

3 Hold a tissue between the spray bottle and the plastic. Spray water on the tissue.

4 **Record** what you see. **Compare** your results.

Think! What did you see that surprised you?

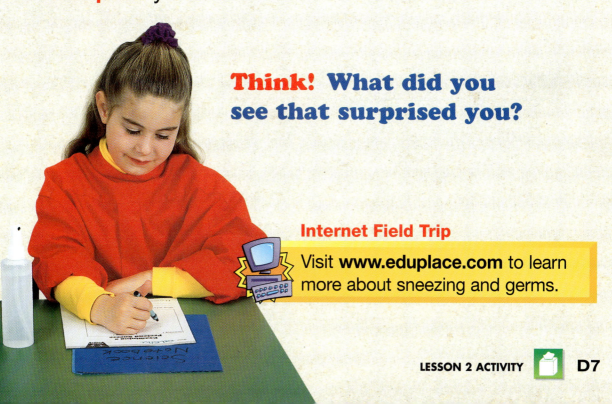

Internet Field Trip

Visit **www.eduplace.com** to learn more about sneezing and germs.

LESSON 2 ACTIVITY   D7

Sneezing Spreads Germs

The picture shows a boy sneezing. It begins with the boy throwing back his head. It ends with the boy sneezing into his hands. As he **sneezes**, air and liquid come out of his nose and mouth. There are germs in the liquid. The large circle shows how these germs look under a microscope.

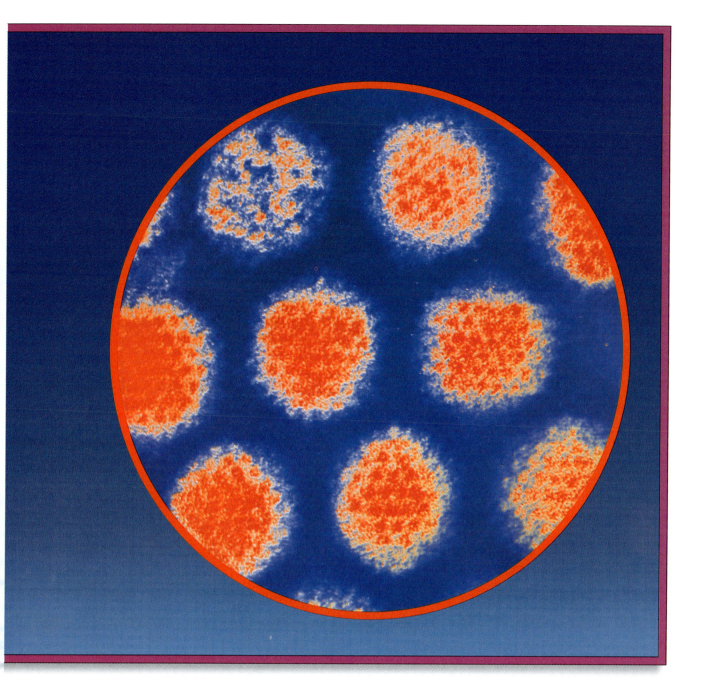

What are some ways to keep germs from spreading when you sneeze? You can cover your nose and mouth with your hands. You can also hold a tissue over your nose and mouth. Remember to put the tissue in the trash. Then use soap and water to wash the germs off your hands.

Reading Check **Write** about how a sneeze spreads germs.

Lesson 3: What are other ways that germs are spread?

Activity

Examining How Germs Travel

What You Need

- piece of stick candy
- goggles
- paper plate
- colored chalk dust
- cup of water
- Science Notebook

1. Dip a piece of candy in water and roll it in chalk dust on a plate.

❷ Roll the candy in your hands.

❸ **Predict** what will happen when you shake hands with a classmate. **Record** your prediction.

Examining How Germs Travel	
Prediction	Result

❹ Shake hands with a classmate. **Record** what happened.

Think! If the chalk dust were germs, in what other ways could germs be spread?

LESSON 3 ACTIVITY   D11

Germs Everywhere

Think about places where you might find germs. Germs can be found almost everywhere. All of the objects in this picture may have germs on them.

Arrows point to places where germs might be. There may be germs on the paper, the eraser, and the pencil. Where else might there be germs?

In the circles you see germs as you would see them under a microscope. The germs look bigger than they really are. Remember, germs are very small.

How might these objects have been covered with germs? A boy with germs on his hands touches the pencil. The germs **spread** to the pencil. Then when another boy touches the same pencil, the germs spread to his hands.

Even though you cannot see germs, you know they are there. How are these children spreading germs?

You know that germs might come from the hands of people when they touch objects. Germs may also come from people who sneeze near objects. If a child sneezes or coughs, germs may spray onto the objects. Then when someone touches the same object, the germs spread to that person's hands.

What are some ways you can keep germs from spreading? You can wash your hands. You can wash things that are touched by many hands. You can cover your nose and mouth with a tissue when you sneeze or cough. You can also keep things that don't belong in your mouth out of your mouth.

✓ **Reading Check** Draw a picture that shows two ways children can spread germs.

Lesson 4: How does your body protect you from germs?

Activity
Examining How Dust Collects

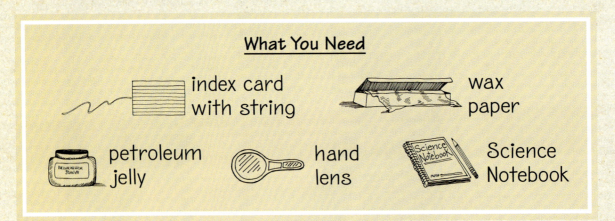

What You Need

- index card with string
- wax paper
- petroleum jelly
- hand lens
- Science Notebook

1 Use wax paper to spread petroleum jelly on an index card.

❷ **Observe** the index card with a hand lens. **Record** what you see.

❸ Hang the card where moving air will blow on it.

❹ *Using Math* Repeat step 2 after two days. **Compare** your results.

Think! Why did the surface of the card change?

Find Out More!

Use a microscope to look at the index cards from all the groups. Which card has the most dust? What does that tell you about germs?

Trapping Germs

Look at the picture of the girl playing baseball. She is kicking up dust as she slides. What are the other children doing? They are also putting dust into the air.

Think about how it feels to breathe when dust is in the air. Dust can make it hard to breathe. Dust has germs in it. So dust puts germs into the air.

Your body protects you from germs. One way is by trapping dust and germs in mucus. **Mucus** is a sticky material in your nose, mouth, and throat.

Mucus helps trap dust and germs to keep them from getting farther into your body. Germs cannot make you sick if they cannot get into your body.

✓ **Reading Check** **Tell** about one way that your body protects you from germs.

UNIT D CHECKPOINT

Word Power

If you need help, turn to the pages shown in blue.

Match a word with a picture. (D4–D5) (D8–D9)

microscope　　sneeze　　germs

1.
2.
3.

Use these words to fill in the blanks.

bacteria　　mucus　　spread　　virus

4. When you pick up an object, germs _____ to your hands. (D12–D13)

5. Small living things that can cause a sore throat are called _____. (D4–D5)

6. A sticky material in your nose, mouth, and throat is called _____. (D18–D19)

7. The germ that causes a cold is called a _____. (D4–D5)

Solving Science Problems

The children in your class keep getting sick. Explain why you think this happens. What are some things you and your classmates can do to stay healthy? Make a plan. Share your plan with your classmates.

WHAT MAKES ME SICK

People Using Science

Lab Technician

When you have a sore throat, a doctor may use a swab to get some germs from your throat. The doctor sends the germs to a lab technician.

A lab technician looks at the germs under a microscope. Then he or she tells the doctor what kind of germs they are.

Why is it helpful to know what kind of germs are in your throat?

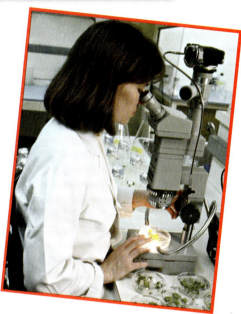

 Guess and Check

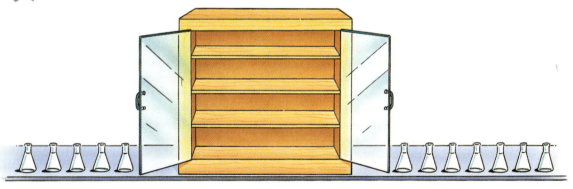

Guess and then use counters to check each answer.

1. Mr. Ortiz has 12 bottles. There are 4 shelves in the cabinet. He wants to put the same number of bottles on each shelf. How many bottles should he put on each shelf?

2. If there were only 3 shelves, how many bottles should Mr. Ortiz put on each shelf?

LESSON 5: How can you prevent the spread of germs?

Activity
Stopping Germs From Spreading

What You Need

Science Notebook

1. **Talk** to your school nurse about germs and how they are spread.

❷ **Find** places in school where germs might be spread. **Record** what you observe.

Stopping Germs From Spreading	
Where germs are spread	My plan

❸ **Make a plan** to help stop the spread of germs in school.

❹ **Record** your plan. Then carry out your plan.

Think! How could you prevent germs from spreading in your home?

Internet Field Trip

Visit **www.eduplace.com** to learn more about ways germs spread.

LESSON 5 ACTIVITY D23

Protect Yourself

Think about how germs might be spread in each picture. The first boy has cut his knee. Germs can get inside his body through the cut. The girls are drinking from the same straw. They are sharing germs. The last boy is about to pick up an apple core. It carries the germs of the person who ate it.

What can be done to keep germs from spreading? The first boy can wash the cut with soap and water. Then he can put a bandage on the cut to keep it clean. Each girl should have her own drink.

The last boy should use a napkin or paper towel to pick up the apple core. He should throw it away in the trash. Then the boy should wash his hands with soap and water.

All of these people are helping to keep germs from spreading.

◀ This girl is washing her hands with soap and water. She is killing the germs on her skin.

This boy washed his cut with soap and water. His mom puts a bandage on it to keep germs out. ▶

◀ This girl keeps her mouth away from the spout. This helps keep germs that are on the spout out of her body.

WHAT MAKES ME SICK

This man is cleaning away germs. He uses a **disinfectant** to help kill the germs. ▼

Using Math Decide if each of the four activities shown takes less than one minute or more than one minute. Record your ideas in a chart like the one below.

Keeping Germs From Spreading	
Less than one minute	More than one minute

✓ **Reading Check** **Act out a story** that shows one way that you can keep germs from spreading.

How can you prevent sickness and injury?

Activity
Examining Health and Safety

What You Need

 crayons

 Science Notebook

1 **Look at** the cartoon strip. **Tell** what happens first, next, and last.

2 **Draw** your own cartoon strip in a chart. First, show someone who is sick or injured.

3 Next, show what could be done to make that person healthy again.

4 Last, show how the sickness or injury could have been prevented.

Examining Health and Safety
First
Next
Last

Think! What can you do at home to prevent sickness and injury?

LESSON 6 ACTIVITY

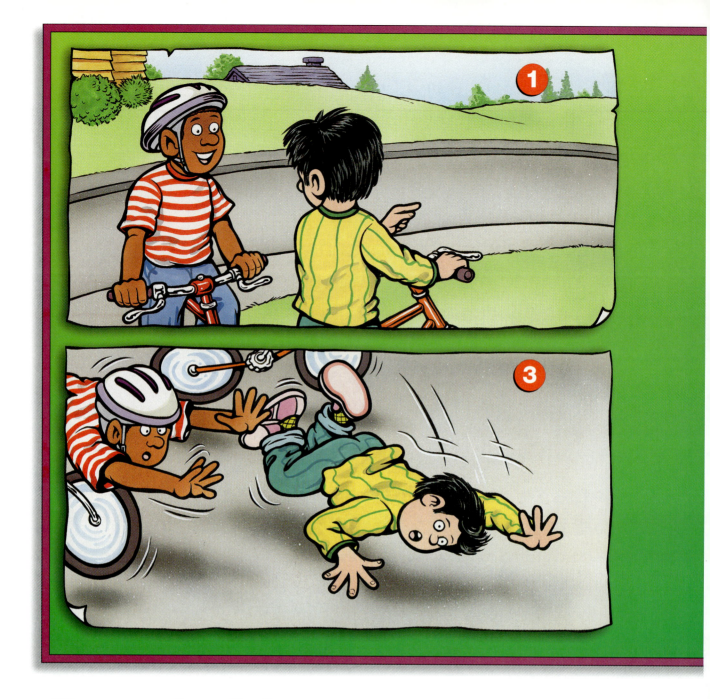

Preventing Injury

Look at the picture story. What happened? One of the boys hit his head on the sidewalk. He has a head **injury**. Why does one boy have a head injury but the other boy does not? The boy that hurt his head was not wearing a **safety helmet**. The boy without the injury was wearing a safety helmet.

The boy who hurt his head can **prevent**, or stop, an injury from happening again. The most important way is to wear a safety helmet.

What else can the boy do to prevent an injury? He can pedal slower. He can be careful to watch where he is going. The boy might even wear elbow pads on his arms and kneepads on his legs. These pads will protect the boy if he falls.

There are many things that you can do to prevent injury. Be careful near the street. Only cross when it is safe. Look both ways to make sure there are no cars. Look for the walk sign if there is one.

When you carry sharp objects, you should walk slowly. You should keep the point away from you and others. When passing scissors, hold the blades and point the handle toward the other person.

You can help prevent injuries when playing sports. A hockey player wears a safety helmet, pads, and special gloves for protection.

You can help prevent injuries when riding in a car. You should stay seated. You should always wear a **seat belt**. Young children should ride in car seats.

✓ **Reading Check** **Write a story** about someone who prevents an injury from happening.

Lesson 7 — How can you stay healthy?

Activity
Exploring Healthful Activities

What You Need

pictures of healthful activities

crayons

Science Notebook

1 **Look at** some pictures of healthful activities. **Talk about** why the activities are healthful.

❷ Think of another healthful activity.

❸ **Draw** a picture of yourself doing that activity.

❹ **Write** about how your activity will help you stay healthy.

Think! What are some other ways you can keep your body healthy?

Find Out More!

What else do you want to know about staying healthy? Ask questions. Make a plan to find answers. Share your findings with your classmates.

Staying Healthy

How can you keep your body healthy? You can eat **healthful foods**. These kinds of foods help your body grow strong. You can also **exercise**. This will make your muscles and bones stronger.

Getting enough sleep helps keep you healthy, too. When you sleep, your body gets the rest it needs.

Too many cookies, candies, or potato chips are not good for you. Alcohol, cigarettes, and drugs are not good for you either.

Follow the maze with your finger. Decide which things are good for your body. You will get to the finish by choosing healthful things.

Reading Check **Draw a picture** to show three ways that you can help your body stay healthy.

UNIT D UNIT REVIEW

Word Power

If you need help, turn to the pages shown in blue.

Match the words with a picture. (D30–D33)

injury   safety helmet   seat belt

1.   2.   3.

Write the letter of the correct words.

4. You wear a safety helmet to _____ an injury. (D30–D31)
   a. prevent   b. sneeze   c. spread   d. exercise

5. A _____ helps you see things that are small. (D4–D5)
   a. injury   b. sneeze   c. germ   d. microscope

6. A _____ helps to kill germs. (D26–D27)
   a. mucus   b. seat belt   c. injury   d. disinfectant

7. Bacteria and viruses are two kinds of _____. (D4–D5)
   a. germs   b. exercises   c. mucus   d. injuries

8. A sticky material that helps keep germs from getting into your body is called _____. (D18–D19)
   a. seat belt   b. bacteria   c. mucus   d. disinfectant

9. You _____ to make your muscles stronger. (D36–D37)
   a. spread   b. exercise   c. prevent   d. sneeze

10. You should eat _____ to help your body grow. (D36–D37)
    a. seat belts   b. viruses   c. bacteria   d. healthful foods

D38   WHAT MAKES ME SICK

Using Science Ideas

How are germs being spread? Make a list.

Writing in Science

Explain how each action helps keep you and others healthy. Share your ideas with your classmates.

1. Washing hands
2. Wearing a safety helmet
3. Using a disinfectant
4. Using a tissue when you sneeze
5. Eating fruit instead of chips

Make a poster. Use words and pictures to show ways to stay healthy.

Main Idea and Details

Matthew likes to keep germs from spreading. When he sneezes, Matthew covers his mouth and nose with a tissue. He puts the tissue in the trash. Then he washes his hands with soap and water. When Matthew gets a cut, he washes it. Then his mother covers the cut with a bandage.

Use the story above to answer the questions.
1. What is the main idea of the story?
2. What are three things that Matthew does to help keep germs from spreading?

Using MATH SKILLS

Find a Pattern

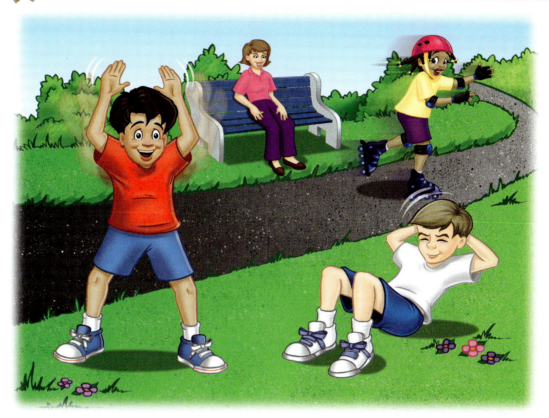

Find each pattern.

1. Alan does sit-ups to stay healthy. On Tuesday he does 5. On Wednesday he does 10. On Thursday he does 15. What is the pattern?

2. Tanya roller-skates to exercise. On her first try, she roller-skates for 10 minutes. On her second try, she skates for 20 minutes. On her third try, she skates for 30 minutes. What is the pattern?

3. Marco does jumping jacks to stay healthy. On Monday he does 7 jumping jacks. On Tuesday he does 17. On Wednesday he does 27. What is the pattern? If he continues this pattern, how many jumping jacks will Marco do on Thursday?

Science and Math Toolbox

Using a Hand Lens H2

Using a Thermometer H3

Using a Ruler H4

Using a Calculator H5

Using a Balance H6

Making a Chart H7

Making a Tally Chart H8

Making a Bar Graph H9

Using a Hand Lens

A hand lens is a tool that makes objects look bigger. It helps you see the small parts of an object.

Look at a Coin

1. Place a coin on your desk.

2. Hold the hand lens above the coin. Look through the lens. Slowly move the lens away from the coin. What do you see?

3. Keep moving the lens away until the coin looks blurry.

4. Then slowly move the lens closer. Stop when the coin does not look blurry.

Using a Thermometer

A thermometer is a tool used to measure temperature. Temperature tells how hot or cold something is. It is measured in degrees.

Find the Temperature of Water

1. Put water into a cup.
2. Put a thermometer into the cup.
3. Watch the colored liquid in the thermometer. What do you see?
4. Look how high the colored liquid is. What number is closest? That is the temperature of the water.

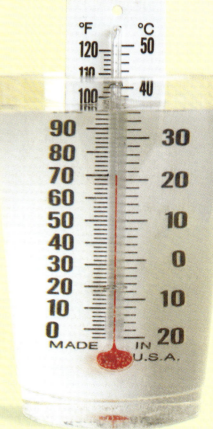

Using a Ruler

A ruler is a tool used to measure the length of objects. Some rulers measure length in inches. Other rulers measure length in centimeters.

Measure a Crayon

1. Place the ruler on your desk.

2. Lay your crayon next to the ruler. Line up one end with the 0 mark on the ruler.

3. Look at the other end of the crayon. Which number is closest to that end?

Using a Calculator

A calculator is a tool that can help you add numbers. It can also help you subtract numbers.

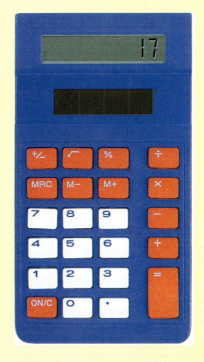

Subtract Numbers

1. Tim and Anna both grew plants.
   Tim grew 8 plants.
   Anna grew 17 plants.

2. How many more plants did Anna grow? Use your calculator to find out.

3. Enter `1` `7` on the calculator. Then press the `−` key. Enter `8` and press `=`.

4. What is your answer?

Using a Balance

A balance is a tool used to measure mass. Mass is the amount of matter in an object.

Measure the Mass of Clay

1. Check that the pointer is on the middle mark of the balance. If needed, move the slider on the back to the left or right.

2. Place a clay ball in one pan.

3. Add masses to the other pan until the pointer is at the middle mark again.

4. Add the numbers on the masses to find the mass in grams of the clay.

5. Add more clay to the ball. Repeat steps 3 and 4. How did the mass change?

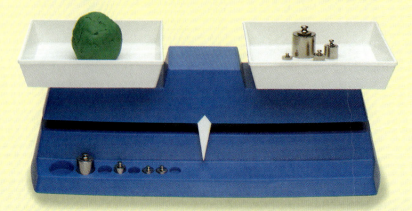

Making a Chart

A chart can help you sort information, or data. When you sort data it is easier to read and compare.

Make a Chart to Compare Animals

1. Give the chart a title.
2. Name the groups that tell about the data you collect.
3. Carefully fill in the data in each column.

How Animals Move	
Animal	How it moves
fish	swim
dog	walk, swim
duck	walk, swim, fly

Which animal can move in the most ways?

Making a Tally Chart

A tally chart helps you keep track of items as you count.

Make a Tally Chart of Kinds of Pets

Jan's class drew pictures of their pets. You can make a tally chart to record the number of each kind of pet.

1. Every time you count one pet, you make one tally.

2. When you get to five, your fifth tally should be a line across the other four.

3. Count the tallies to find each total.

Kinds of Pets		
Pet	Tally	Total
Bird	III	3
Dog	ℋ I	6
Fish	I	1

How many of each kind of pet do the children have?

Making a Bar Graph

A bar graph can help you sort and compare data.

Make a Bar Graph of Favorite Leaves

You can use the data in the tally chart to make a bar graph.

1. Choose a title for your graph.
2. Write numbers along the side.
3. Write leaf names along the bottom.
4. Start at the bottom of each column. Fill in one box for each tally.

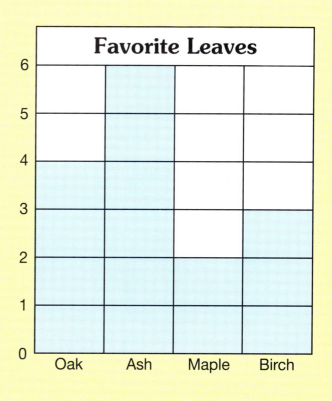

Favorite Leaves		
Leaf	Tally	Total
Oak	IIII	4
Ash	IIII I	6
Maple	II	2
Birch	III	3

Which leaf is the favorite?

GLOSSARY

adapt To change in order to live in a certain habitat. A plant can adapt to dark habitats by growing towards light. (A38)

adult The last stage in a life cycle. Baby animals grow and change to become adult animals. (A5)

bacteria Tiny living things that can only be seen with a microscope. Some bacteria cause sickness. (D4)

boulder A very large rock. Boulders can break down into smaller rocks. (C26)

clay soil Soil that has a lot of clay in it. Clay soil sometimes is found below topsoil. (C5)

cone The part of some nonflowering plants where seeds grow. Seeds grow between the scales of a cone. (A24)

disinfectant A material that kills germs. Cleaning with a disinfectant helps prevent the spread of germs. (D27)

egg The first stage in the life cycle of most animals. Some animal babies grow from eggs inside the mother's body. (A10)

erosion The washing away of the land. The roots of trees can help stop erosion. (C32)

exercise Moving your body. Playing outdoors is exercise that helps make your muscles and bones stronger. (D36)

flower A part of some plants. Seeds form in a flower. (A24)

force A push or a pull. A force can cause an object to move, stop, or change direction. (B24)

fossil remains What is left of a plant or an animal that lived long ago. Some dinosaur bones may become fossil remains. (C42)

fruit A part of a flower that grows around seeds. Fruits protect the seeds inside of them. (A29)

germ A tiny living thing that can make you sick. Bacteria and viruses are two kinds of germs. (D4)

gravity A force that pulls objects toward the earth. When a frog jumps, gravity pulls it back down to the earth. (A39, B27)

hatch When a baby animal breaks out of an egg that grew outside its mother's body. Baby chicks and some snakes hatch from eggs. (A10)

healthful foods Foods that are good for your body. Fruits, vegetables, breads, milk, and fish are healthful foods. (D36)

heat A form of energy used to warm things up. Heat is made by rubbing, burning, and light from the sun. (B42)

inherit To have traits passed on from one's parents. A cat inherits its fur and its body shape from its parents. (A18)

injury Something harmful that happens to a person. Some injuries are cuts, scrapes, bruises, and broken bones. (D30)

learned Behaviors that are not inherited from parents. Riding a bicycle is something that is learned. (A19)

lens A piece of transparent glass or plastic that brings together or spreads rays of light. A lens can make an object look bigger or smaller. (B16)

life cycle The order of changes that a living thing goes through during its lifetime. The life cycle of a frog is different from the life cycle of a butterfly. (A4)

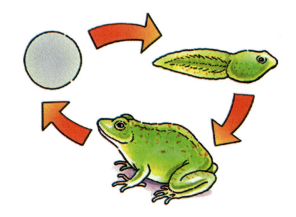

life span The length of time between birth or hatching and death. (A25)

light A form of energy that you can see. Light from a flashlight travels in a straight line. (B4)

living thing Something that is alive and can grow. Living things need food, water, and air. (C9)

microscope A tool that makes small things appear larger. Most germs can be seen with the aid of a microscope. (D5)

mineral Nonliving materials formed in the earth. Rocks contain one or more minerals. (C36)

motion Moving from one place to another. When something is in motion, it changes its position. (B20)

mucus A sticky material that traps germs and dust. Mucus in your nose, mouth, and throat help protect your body from germs. (D19)

natural resource A material found in or on the earth that people use. Water, oil, gas, and trees are natural resources. (B46)

nonliving thing Something that was never alive. A rock is a nonliving thing. (C9)

O

once-living thing Something that was alive at one time or was once part of a living thing. A log is an example of a once-living thing. (C8)

opaque Keeping light from passing through. An opaque object casts a shadow. The human body and a paper bag are both opaque. (B10)

P

pitch How high or low a sound is. The pitch of a gong is low. (B36)

pollen A powdery material made by one part of a flower. When pollen lands on eggs inside the flower, seeds may form. (A28)

prevent To keep from happening. Wearing a safety helmet when skating can help prevent injury. (D31)

puddle A small pool of water. Water from puddles can soak into the soil. (C14)

R

reflect To throw back. A mirror reflects light. The moon reflects the light of the sun. (B6)

rock Nonliving thing that can break down to form soil. Rocks are found under soil, under oceans, and under other rocks. (C4)

---- **S** ----

safety helmet A hard covering to protect the head. It is a good idea to wear a safety helmet when riding a bike. (D30)

sand Very small rocks. Some ocean beaches are covered with sand. (C27)

sandy soil Soil that is made of very small rocks. Sandy soil can be found near oceans and lakes. (C5)

scratch To make a mark on something. A hard mineral can scratch a soft mineral. (C38)

seat belt A strap to hold a person in place while riding in a car. Wearing a seat belt can help prevent injuries. (D33)

seed The beginning of a plant. Plants grow from seeds. (A24)

seed coat The outside shell around a seed. The seed coat protects the seed. (A34)

shadow A dark shape formed when an object blocks light. Shadows can change when the object moves. (B13)

shelter A place to live. A home is a shelter where people can rest and be safe. (C18)

sneeze A sudden forcing of breath through the nose and mouth. Sneezing is one way that germs are spread. (D8)

sound Waves of vibration that you hear. Waves vibrate faster for high sounds than for low sounds. (B33)

speed How fast an object moves. The speed of a dog running is greater than the speed of a turtle walking. (B21)

spread To pass from one person to another. Diseases are spread by sneezing, coughing, and touching objects that have germs on them. (D13)

stage Step in the life cycle of a living thing. An egg is the first stage in the life cycle of most animals. (A4)

texture The way something feels. Rough and smooth are textures. (C36)

topsoil A top layer of dark, loose soil. Most plants grow well in topsoil. (C5)

trace fossil The imprint of a once-living thing. Dinosaur footprints in rock are one kind of trace fossil. (C42)

translucent Allowing some light to pass through. Some translucent objects are frosted glass and wax paper. (B10)

transparent Allowing light to pass through. Clear water and plastic wrap are transparent. (B10)

vibration Fast motion back and forth. You can see the vibration of a guitar string if you pluck it. (B32)

virus A very small germ that causes sickness. You need a very powerful microscope to see a virus. (D5)

volume The loudness of a sound. The volume control on a telephone can be used to make the volume louder or softer. (B37)

wave An up-and-down or back-and-forth motion. Water moves in waves on the ocean. Sound moves in waves through the air. (B32)

weathering The breaking up or wearing away of rocks. Wind, water, and plants can weather rocks. (C30)

H17

INDEX

A
Alcohol, D37
Animals
    adult, A5–A7
    baby, A5–A7
    life cycles of, A2–A15

B
Bacteria, D4
Birds, life cycles of, A10–A11
Bones, D36
Boulders C26–C27
Burning, and heat, B43
Butterfly, A14–A15

C
Cigarettes, D37
Clay soil, C2–C5,
    C12–C13, C14
Cones, A24

Conservation, B47
Cough, D14–D15

D
Direction
    and forces, B25
    and light, B3, B6–B7, B16
Disinfectant, D27
Distance, B19, B21
Drugs, D37
Dust, D10–D11, D16–D19

E
Earth
    and gravity, B27
Eggs
    bird, A10–A11
    caterpillar, A14–A15
    chicken, A8–A9
    differences in, A8–A9, A10
    examining, A8–A9

frog, A14–A15
hatching from, A10–A11, A14–A15
in plants, A28
salmon, A8–A9

Erosion
prevention of, C33
of rock, C32
of soil, C33

Exercise, D36

F

Flashlight tag, B4–B7
Flowers, A24–A29, A45
examining, A26–A27
and fruit, A29
and seeds, A24, A28–A29
Forces, B24–B27
Forest fires, A50–A51
Fossils, C40–C45
formation of, C42–C43
Fossil remains, C42–C45, C48
of dinosaurs, C42–C45
of trees, C44
Frogs, A6–A7, A14–A15, A54
Fruits, A24–A31, A42–A43

G

Germs, D4–D5, D7, D18–D19
models of, D2–D3
preventing spread of, D15, D22–D27
spreading of, D8–D9, D10–D15, D24
Goldfish, A16–A17
Gravity, A39, B27

H

Hardness of rocks, C34–C35, C38–C39
Hatching, A10
Health, maintaining good, D34–D37
Healthful foods, D36
Heat
and light, B43
making, B40–B43, B46–B47
and motion, B40–B42
saving, B44–B45

I

Inherited traits
of animals, A18–A19
of plants, A30–A31

Injury, D28–D33

L

Learned behavior, A16–A19
Lenses, B14–B17
Life cycles
    animal, A2–A11, A54
    differences in, A12–A15
    effects on, A50–A51
    plant, A22–A31
Life spans, A25
Light
    bending, B3, B16
    from electric bulb, B5
    and heat, B43
    and lens, B16
    movement of, B4–B7
    observing, B8–B9
    and opaque objects,
        B10–B13
    path of, B2–B4
    reflected, B6–B7
    and translucent objects,
        B10–B13
    and transparent objects,
        B10–B13, B16

Living things, C8–C11, C15
    changes in, A4–A5
    inherited traits of, A16–A19
    learned behavior of,
        A16–A19
Loudness, B37

M

Machines, used to move
    objects, B26
Magnets, and force, B26
Mealworms, A12–A13
Measuring
    motion, B18–B19, B21
Microscope, D2–D3, D5, D8,
    D13, D17
Minerals, C36–C37
    grouping, C46–C49
    hardness of, C34–C35,
        C38–C39
    kinds of, C37–C39
    uses of, C50–C53
Mirror, and light, B3, B6–B7
Motion
    and forces, B24–B27
    and heat, B40–B42

kinds of, B20
and magnet, B23, B26
measuring, B18–B19, B21
observing, B30–B31
and position, B20
and vibration, B32–B33
and waves, B32–B33
Mouse, A14–A15
Mouth, D8–D9, D15, D19, D26
Mucus, D19

N
Natural resources, B46–B47
Needs, of plants, A38–A39
Nonliving things, C8–C11

O
Once-living things, C8–C11, C14, C42
Opaque objects, B10–B13

P
Pansy, life cycle of, A24
Pine, life cycle of, A25
Pitch, B36, B39

Plants
and frost, A40
and gravity, A39
inherited traits of, A30–A31
life cycles of, A22–A25
life spans of, A5
and light, A38, A41
parts of, A24, A26–A31
and touch, A40
uses of, C16–C21
and wind, A40
Pollen, A28
Preventing, D28–D33
Puddles, C14–C15
Pull, B23, B24, B26–B27
Push, B20, B22–B27

R
Reflection
light, B6–B7
Rocks
and erosion, C32–C33
as fossils, C42–C43
grouping, C46–C49
hardness of, C34–C35
and minerals, C36–C37

sizes of, C24–C27
in soil, C4–C5, C8–C11
uses of, C50–C53
and weathering, C28–C31, C33
Roots, C4–C5, C33

S

Safety, D28–D33
Safety helmet, D30–D31, D33
Sand, C26–C27, C28–C29
Sandy soil, C2–C5, C12–C14
Scratch, rocks, C38–C39
Scientific methods (Think Like a Scientist), S2–S7
   hypothesis, S4
   test, S5
Seat belt, D33
Seed coat, A34
Seeds, A24–A35
   and animals, A35
   examining, A32–A33
   kinds of, A34–A35
   and wind, A35
Shadow, B13
Shelter, B46, C18
Sickness, D4, D29
Sizes, of rocks, C24–C27
Sleep, D36
Sneezing, D6–D9, D14–D15
Soil
   analyzing, C6–C11
   kinds of, C2–C5
   layers of, C4–C5
   uses of, C16–C21
   and water, C12–C15
Sound(s)
   high and low, B34–B36
   loud and soft, B36–B39
   observing, B30–B31
   vibration, B32–B33, B36
   volume, B37–B39
   waves, B32–B33, B35
Speed, B21, B24–B25
Spread, disease, D13
Stages
   in animal life cycles, A4, A8–A11
   in plant life cycles, A22–A25
Sun
   and heat, B43

T

Tadpoles, A6–A7, A54
Teeth, D4
Temperature, B45
Texture
 of rocks and minerals,
  C36–C37, C49
Thermometer, B44–B45
Topsoil, C2–C5, C12–C13,
 C14
Trace fossils, C42–C45, C48
Translucent objects, B10–B13
Transparent objects,
 B10–B13, B16
Tuning fork, B30–B31

V

Vibration, B32–B33, B36

Virus, D4–D5
Volume, B37–B39

W

Water
 as lens, B14–B17
 moving, C28–C29,
  C32–C33
 in soil, C12–C15
 uses of, C16–C21
Waves, sound, B32–B33, B35
Weathering
 and plants, C31
 of rocks, C30–C31, C33
 and water, C30
 and wind, C31

CREDITS

ILLUSTRATORS
Cover Ruth Flanigan.

Think Like a Scientist 2–7: Steven Carpenter. 10–11: Laurie Hamilton. *border* Ruth Flanigan.

Unit A 4–7: Richard Courtney. 14: George Ulrich. 18: Charles Jordon. 20: *t.* Tom Pansini, *b.* Karen Lee Schmidt. 24: Lori Anzalone. 25: Dan McGowan. 52: Tom Pansini. 54: Bernard Adnet. 55: Tom Pansini.

Unit B 4–7: John Ceballos. 28–29: Tom Pansini. 36–39: Tate Nation. 42–43: Mike Dammer. 48: TomPansini. 49: Mike Dammer. 51: Patrick Girouard.

Unit C 4: Lori Anzalone. 14, 15: Robert Roper. 18–19: Michael Reid. 22: Tom Pansini. 23: Sharon Hawkins Vargo. 45: Jenny Campbell. 54: Tom Pansini.

Unit D 20–21: Tom Pansini. 28–29: Eldon Doty. 30–31: Jerry Zimmerman. 36–37: Jenny Campbell. 38–39: Tom Pansini. 40–41: Mark McIntyre.

Science and Math Toolbox *logos* Nancy Tobin. 5: Randy Verougstraete. 7–8: Randy Chewning. 10: Randy Verougstraete. *border* Ruth Flanigan.

Glossary 10–18: Tom Pansini.

Extra Practice Laurie Hamilton.

PHOTOGRAPHS

All photographs by Houghton Mifflin Company (HMCo.) unless otherwise noted.

Cover *t.* David Phillips/Visuals Unlimited; *m.l.* Picture Perfect USA; *b.r.* Guy Grenier/Masterfile Corporation.

Unit A 1: *l.* © Norm Thomas/Photo Researchers, Inc.; *m.* © E.R. Degginger/Photo Researchers, Inc.; *r.* © Alan & Linda Detrick/Photo Researchers, Inc. 10: *l.* Tim Wright/Corbis; *t.r.* Hal H. Harrison/Grant Heilman Photography, Inc.; *b.r.* Jennifer Loomis/Animals Animals/Earth Scenes. 10–11: IFA/Bruce Coleman Inc. 11: *t.* Michael Habicht/Animals Animals/Earth Scenes; *b.* Marcia W. Griffen/Animals Animals/Earth Scenes. 14: *t.l.* Dwight R. Kuhn; *t.r.* Dwight R. Kuhn; *m.l.* © E.R. Degginger/Photo Researchers, Inc.; *m.r.* © Norm Thomas/Photo Researchers, Inc.; *b.l.* E.R. Degginger/Color-Pic, Inc.; *b.r.* E.R. Degginger/Color-Pic, Inc. 15: *t.l.* Dwight R. Kuhn; *t.m.* Dwight R. Kuhn; *t.r.* Breck P. Kent/Animals Animals/Earth Scenes; *m.l.* © Steve Ross/Photo Researchers, Inc.; *m.m.* © E.R. Degginger/Photo Researchers, Inc.; *m.r.* © Alan & Linda Detrick/Photo Researchers, Inc.; *b.l.* E.R. Degginger/Color-Pic, Inc.; *b.m.* E.R. Degginger/Color-Pic, Inc.; *b.r.* E.R. Degginger/Color-Pic, Inc. 21: The Seeing Eye, Inc. 28: *bkgd.* © Hans Reinhard/OKAPIA/Photo Researchers, Inc.; *inset* © Holt Studios International (Nigel Cattlin)/Photo Researchers, Inc. 29: *bkgd.* John Tinning/Frank Lane Picture Agency/Corbis; *inset* John Colwell/Grant Heilman Photography, Inc. 30–31: *bkgd.* Larry Lefever/Grant Heilman Photography, Inc. 34: *t. inset* Gordon R. Gainer/The Stock Market; *b. inset* Dwight R. Kuhn. 35: *t. inset* Dwight R. Kuhn; *b.l. inset* © S.E. Cornelius/Photo Researchers, Inc.; *b.r. inset* E.R. Degginger/Color-Pic, Inc. 37: *t.* Grant Huntington for HMCo.; *m.* Grant Huntington for HMCo. 38: Barry L. Runk/Grant Heilman Photography, Inc. 39: Dwight R. Kuhn. 40: *t.* Runk/Schoenberger/Grant Heilman Photography, Inc.; *m.* Dwight R. Kuhn; *b.* Richard Shiell/Animals Animals/Earth Scenes. 41: Larry Lefever/Grant Heilman Photography, Inc. 44: *t.l.* Jane Grushow/Grant Heilman Photography, Inc.; *b.l.* Eric Crichton/Corbis; *t.r.* Tania Midgley/Corbis; *b.r.* Jim Strawser/Grant Heilman Photography, Inc. 45: *t.l.* Eric Crichton/Corbis; *t.r.* Jane Grushow/Grant Heilman Photography, Inc.; *b.l.* Jane Grushow/Grant Heilman Photography, Inc.; *b.r.* Tania Midgley/Corbis. 50: Mugshots 1997/The Stock Market. 53: © Fred Whitehead/Animals Animals/Earth Scenes.

Unit B B: *l.* John De Visser/Masterfile Corporation; *r.* Richard V. Procopio/Stock Boston. 1: Jerome Prevost-TempSport/Corbis. 10–13: Superstock. 20: *t.* B. Daemmrich/The Image Works Inc. 20–21: *bkgd.* PhotoDisc, Inc; *inset* Jerome Prevost-TempSport/Corbis. 21: *l.* Neil Preston/Corbis; *r.* Luongo/The Gamma Liaison Network.

26: *m.* E.R. Degginger/Color-Pic, Inc.; *b* Matt Bradley/Tom Stack & Associates. 26–27: Phil Degginger/Color-Pic, Inc. 27: Jack Vartoogian Photography. 32: *inset* James H. Karales/Peter Arnold, Inc. 33: Richard Gross/The Stock Market. 46: *b.l.* Anthony Redpath/The Stock Market; *b.r.* John De Visser/Masterfile Corporation. 47: *b.* Richard V. Procopio/Stock Boston.

Unit C 1: © Dale Sanders/Masterfile. 20: *t.l.* © Holt Studios Ltd./Photo Researchers, Inc.; *b.l.* Grant Heilman Photography, Inc.; *b.r.* Corbis. 21: *t.l.* David Muench/Corbis; *b.l.* Mark E. Gibson/Mark and Audra Gibson Photography; *b.r.* David Young-Wolff/PhotoEdit. 22: E.R. Degginger/Color-Pic, Inc. 23: Anne Kuhn/Dwight R. Kuhn. 26–27: Superstock. 27: Parvinder S. Sethi. 30: Dave Bartruff/Corbis. 30–31: © Charlie Ott/Photo Researchers, Inc. 31: © William E. Ferguson. 32: Wayne Lankinen/DRK Photo. 33: Superstock. 36–37: Jerry Jacka Photography. 37: *t.r.* E.R. Degginger/Color-Pic, Inc.; *b.l.* David R. Frazier Photography; *b.m.* © Ben Simmons/The Stock Market. 38: *t.l.* Steven Frisch/Stock Boston; *m.r.* E.R. Degginger/Color-Pic, Inc.; *b.l.* E.R. Degginger/Color-Pic, Inc. 39: *t.r.* E.R. Degginger/Color-Pic, Inc. 42: © Francois Gohier/Photo Researchers, Inc. 43: *l.* Tom & Susan Bean, Inc.; *r.* Courtesy, Peter Gregg. 44: *t.* Jonathan Blair/Woodfin Camp & Associates; *m.* Michael Fogden/Michael and Patricia Fogden; *b.* Breck P. Kent. 45: Breck P. Kent Photography. 52–53: © Dale Sanders/Masterfile. 53: *t.* Craig Lovell/Eagle Visions Photography; *b.* Madeline Polss/Envision.

Unit D D: *l.* © CDC/Science Source/Photo Researchers, Inc.; *r.* © CNRI/Science Photo Library/Photo Researchers, Inc. 1: *t.l.* © Biophoto Associates/Science Source/Photo Researchers, Inc.; *b.* © Michael Abbey/Photo Researchers, Inc.; *t.r.* © CNRI/Science Photo Library/Photo Researchers, Inc. 4: *t.* © CNRI/Science Photo Library/Photo Researchers, Inc.; *m.* © Michael Abbey/Photo Researchers, Inc.; *b.* © Biophoto Associates/Science Source/Photo Researchers, Inc. 5: *t.r.* © CDC/Science Source/Photo Researchers, Inc.; *b.r.* © CNRI/Science Photo Library/Photo Researchers, Inc. 8: © Globus Brothers. 9: © P. Hawtin/University of Southampton/Science Photo Library/Photo Researchers, Inc. 12: *l.* © David M. Phillips/Photo Researchers, Inc.; *r.* © CNRI/Science Photo Library/Photo Researchers, Inc. 13: © NIBSC/Science Photo Library/Photo Researchers, Inc. 14: Mary Kate Denny/PhotoEdit. 18–19: David Phillips for HMCo. 21: Liane Enkelis/Stock Boston. 24–25: Grant Huntington for HMCo. 26: David Young-Wolff/PhotoEdit. 27: Richard Hutchings for HMCo. 32: *l.* D. Young-Wolff/PhotoEdit. 33: *l.* Mark Gamba/The Stock Market; *r.* Valerie Santagto for HMCo.

Extra Practice

On the following pages are questions about each of the Units in your book. Use these questions to help you review some of the terms and ideas that you studied. Write your answers on a separate sheet of paper.

Contents

Unit A Life Cycles R2

Unit B Energy and Motion R4

Unit C Earth's Materials R6

Unit D What Makes Me Sick R8

Extra Practice

UNIT A Life Cycles

Word Power

Match each word with a picture.

seed   flower   cone

1.
2.
3.

Write the letter of the correct words.

4. The stages in the life of a living thing are called its _____.
   a. adult   **b.** life cycle   **c.** seed coat   **d.** pollen

5. A plant's roots are pulled down by _____.
   a. gravity   **b.** life span   **c.** pollen   **d.** cone

6. The outside shell on a seed is a _____.
   a. pollen   **b.** flower   **c.** seed coat   **d.** cone

Use these words to fill in the blanks.

eggs   adapt   adult   fruit

7. A _____ protects the seeds inside it.
8. Plants _____ to the place where they live.
9. Most animals start their lives as _____.
10. Baby deer grow up to be _____ deer.

Extra Practice

Using Science Ideas

Write each answer.

1. Tell about the life cycle of the dandelion.

2. Jamie said that he saw a baby robin hatch. Tell what he saw.
3. Choose a baby animal. Name three things the baby animal might inherit from its parents.
4. Choose a baby animal. Name three things that the baby animal might learn from its environment.

Extra Practice

UNIT B Energy and Motion

Word Power

Use these words to fill in the blanks.

shadow   transparent   translucent   opaque

1. Light does not pass through _____ objects.
2. If you stand in front of a light, you make a _____.
3. Light passes through _____ objects.
4. Objects that let some light through are _____.

Write the letter of the answer to the riddle.

5. I tell the loudness of sound.
   a. vibration   **b.** pitch   **c.** volume   **d.** gravity

6. I am a wave that you can hear.
   a. gravity   **b.** volume   **c.** sound   **d.** motion

7. I tell how high or low a sound is.
   a. pitch   **b.** volume   **c.** speed   **d.** shadow

8. I am the force that pulls you toward the earth.
   a. vibration   **b.** gravity   **c.** wave   **d.** motion

9. I tell how fast an animal can run.
   a. gravity   **b.** speed   **c.** motion   **d.** pitch

10. I am a back-and-forth motion.
    a. vibration   **b.** pitch   **c.** shadow   **d.** volume

Extra Practice

Using Science Ideas

Write each answer.

1. Order these sounds from softest to loudest.

2. How can you tell if a ball is in motion?
3. Name some ways that heat is made.
4. In what ways can forces change an object's motion?

Extra Practice

UNIT C Earth's Materials

Word Power

Match the words with a picture.

living thing   once-living thing   nonliving thing

1.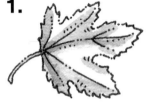
2.
3.

Use these words to answer the riddles.

sand   trace fossils   boulders   fossil remains

4. We are very big rocks.
5. We are once-living things that have changed to rock.
6. We are tiny pieces of broken rock.
7. We are outlines in rocks showing once-living things.

Write the letter of the correct word.

8. When wind and water break rocks, it is called _____.
   a. erosion   b. weathering   c. clay   d. topsoil

9. When there is more water than the soil can hold, _____ are formed.
   a. fossils   b. minerals   c. boulders   d. puddles

10. The feel of a rock is its _____.
    a. texture   b. minerals   c. topsoil   d. growth

Extra Practice

Using Science Ideas

Write each answer.

1. Look at the picture. Name some ways people use plants and water.

2. Suppose you have two kinds of minerals. How can you tell which is harder?

3. Why do people need shelter?

4. How are rocks and minerals useful in our lives?

Extra Practice

UNIT D What Makes Me Sick

Word Power

Match the words with a picture.

exercise   safety helmet   seat belt

1.
2.
3.

Use these words to answer the riddles.

bacteria   mucus   virus   healthful food

4. I am a sticky material inside your nose that traps dust and germs.
5. I am a germ that causes the flu.
6. I am a germ that causes tooth decay.
7. I help your body grow strong.

Write the letter of the correct words.

8. Your muscles and bones grow stronger when you _____.
   a. exercise   b. sneeze   c. injury   d. spread

9. You can use a _____ to kill germs.
   a. microscope   b. disinfectant   c. seat belt   d. virus

10. A football player wears a helmet to prevent _____.
    a. germs   b. spread   c. exercise   d. injury

Extra Practice

Using Science Ideas

Write each answer.

1. How can you help prevent injuries when you go skating?

2. What can you do to keep germs from spreading when you sneeze?

3. Tell how to pass scissors to a friend.

4. Why is dust harmful?